The Mission of God and You

THE

Mission of God and You

Created, Called, and
Commissioned for Something
Bigger than You

Lori McDaniel

THOM S. RAINER, SERIES EDITOR

TYNDALE
MOMENTUM®

A Tyndale nonfiction imprint

Visit Tyndale online at tyndale.com.

Visit Tyndale Momentum online at tyndalemomentum.com.

Tyndale, Tyndale's quill logo, *Tyndale Momentum*, and the Tyndale Momentum logo are registered trademarks of Tyndale House Ministries. Tyndale Momentum is a nonfiction imprint of Tyndale House Publishers, Carol Stream, Illinois.

The Mission of God and You: Created, Called, and Commissioned for Something Bigger than You

Unless otherwise indicated, all Scripture quotations are taken from the *Holy Bible*, New Living Translation, copyright © 1996, 2004, 2015 by Tyndale House Foundation. Used by permission of Tyndale House Publishers, Carol Stream, Illinois 60188. All rights reserved.

Scripture quotations marked NIV are taken from the Holy Bible, *New International Version,*® *NIV.*® Copyright © 1973, 1978, 1984, 2011 by Biblica, Inc.® Used by permission. All rights reserved worldwide.

Scripture quotations marked ESV are from The ESV® Bible (The Holy Bible, English Standard Version®), copyright © 2001 by Crossway, a publishing ministry of Good News Publishers. Used by permission. All rights reserved.

For information about special discounts for bulk purchases, please contact Tyndale House Publishers at csresponse@tyndale.com, or call 1-855-277-9400.

Library of Congress Cataloging-in-Publication Data

A catalog record for this book is available from the Library of Congress.

ISBN 978-1-4964-7380-6

Printed in the United States of America

29	28	27	26	25	24	23
7	6	5	4	3	2	1

To my grandchildren—
two who have just learned to walk,
one learning to crawl,
one who is giving first smiles,
and the others who have yet to be born—
this is for you.

As you grow and learn new things, always keep an open
Bible, an open map, open hands, and an open heart. For you
were created to be a part of something bigger than you!

Contents

Introduction

You're Part of Something Bigger than You

*I knew no one who had what I wanted; in fact I did not
know what I did want. But I knew that if what I had was
all the Christianity there was, the thing was a fraud.*

OSWALD CHAMBERS

IT WAS NOT WHAT I'D EXPECTED, but it was the jolt my soul needed.

I was sitting on a tarp-covered dirt floor in a fledgling village
church in South Asia. The air was thick with the smell of curry
and sweat, and the sound of worship filled the space. Each believer
gathered had been challenged in a previous meeting to share the
gospel with thirty people over the next month, and now they were
testifying to how God had worked as they obediently (and illegally,
in their nation) shared Jesus' salvation with others.[1]

"I shared the gospel with eighteen people—seven became
Christ followers, four want to hear more, two were baptized, and
God healed a woman who couldn't walk."

"I shared the gospel with twenty-six people—four were baptized, two were healed of demon possession, and five are meeting
nightly in my home for prayer."

"I shared the gospel with nineteen. . . . I shared the gospel with twenty-nine. . . . I shared the gospel, and God . . ." The chorus continued around the room until everyone had added a verse.

I'm guessing you're not accustomed to hearing reports like these in your church. Me neither. In comfortable and predictable North American church gatherings, we sing about faith that moves mountains, and we are encouraged to share the gospel, but these believers risked it all to do so. They dared mountains to move and witnessed the landscape of eternity change for many of their families and friends.[2]

Astounded by their reports, I jotted down the numbers. In one month, this embryonic group of fifteen believers shared the gospel with more than three hundred people.[3]

As they celebrated and prayed, their words echoed those of the early church: "Lord, look upon their threats and grant to your servants to *continue to speak your word with all boldness,* while you stretch out your hand to heal, and signs and wonders are performed through the name of your holy servant Jesus."[4]

Their Bible-sized, audacious faith confronted my neatly packaged, cautious faith, and I wanted what they had! Their obedience seemed almost radical, but according to Scripture, it was normal Christ-follower behavior. There was just one disturbing reality—it wasn't *my* normal. It wasn't *my church's* normal. I suspect it's not *your* normal either. But why? Shouldn't it be? Shouldn't the overwhelming love of Christ poured into us by his Spirit compel us at all costs to align our lives and all our ambitions to participate in his mission?[5]

We need our hearts jolted. God's glory is too great. Eternity is too real. Lostness is too vast. And the task is too urgent for us to be unbothered about this.

A Purpose for You That's Bigger than You

You are part of something bigger than you! God's mission is to make his name and his glory known in all the earth. In love, he chose you and set you apart to play a unique part in that mission.

> Its purpose is immeasurable,
> its story is biblical,
> its message is critical,
> its plan is possible,
> its activity is radical,
> its scope is global,
> its movement is unstoppable,
> its span is historical, and
> its value is eternal.

These phrases that characterize the mission of God also outline the trajectory of this book. You'll discover (or perhaps rediscover) that while your life may be small—wait, let me restate that—while your life *is* small, God created you to play a part in a grand purpose. It involves you, but it isn't about you. You are part of something for, and only for, God's glory. God is unwaveringly passionate about his glory and committed to act for the sake of his name in all the earth. This is his mission.

God is our message. He is our motivation. Collectively, his mission is the vision of the church. Individually, his mission shapes the life ambition of every believer.

In the chapters that follow, we will unpack the centrality of God's glory, but for now, let us begin by affirming that *God is worthy* of worship and deserves and desires praise not from just a few people in the world, but "from every nation, from all tribes and peoples and languages."[6]

Mission Is What the Bible Is All About

God's mission is one of the most purpose-filled biblical realities we must grasp as disciples of Christ and as leaders in the church. Yet we sometimes act as if it's optional rather than foundational to the entire Bible and essential for every follower of Jesus.

I grew up in church memorizing the Great Commission (Matthew 28:19-20) and giving pocket change to VBS missions offerings. But when missionaries came to our church to speak about people whose names I couldn't pronounce and who lived in places I couldn't pinpoint on a map, I skipped the service. I believed the Great Commission was a *good thing*; it just wasn't *my thing*.

In a 2022 Barna survey, US Christians were asked, "Have you ever heard of the Great Commission?" The responses were not encouraging. Almost two out of three (63 percent) said no. When asked to identify the Great Commission from a list of five verses, only one in three did so correctly.[7]

Perhaps this describes your church as well. The church, the agent of God's mission, is in a precarious place when its people do not understand the purpose for which it exists and dismiss themselves from having any role in it.

Many followers of Christ have a fragmented view of God's mission based on a few segments of Scripture and snippets of Bible stories. Bible scholar Christopher Wright riddled it this way:

Think of a doctrine—any doctrine between 200 and 2000 (AD). Multiply it by historic confessions. Divide by denominational variations. Add a suspicion of heresy. Subtract the doctrine you first thought of. And what are you left with? Probably just about the sum of what theology and mission have in common in the mind of your average Christian—not much.[8]

God's mission is the thread that holds together the fabric of all Scripture. Pull out that thread, and the meaning of love, peace, grace, mercy, forgiveness, and so much more all unravels. Together, let's trace this thread and see God's redemptive mission throughout the metanarrative of Scripture. It's possible that as we do, you'll find yourself thinking, *Why have I not seen the thread of God's mission before?* and together, we will conclude that "*mission* is what the Bible is all about."[9]

A Mindset Shift Is Essential

When my boys were young, they could turn a stick into anything they imagined—a sword to fight off dragons or a lightsaber to battle Darth Vader. To our dog, that same stick was a chew toy. To my husband, it was an annoying impediment to mowing the yard. Perspective is everything.

When God invited Moses to participate with him in delivering the Israelites from slavery, Moses initially argued with God. He reasoned that his personal inadequacies would make it impossible for the plan to succeed. God didn't validate Moses' self-assessment; instead, he helped him shift his mindset, using the stick Moses held in his hand.

Then the LORD asked him, "What is that in your hand?"

"A shepherd's staff," Moses replied.

"Throw it down on the ground," the LORD told him. So Moses threw down the staff, and it turned into a snake! Moses jumped back.

Then the LORD told him, "Reach out and grab its tail."[10]

The passage doesn't indicate that Moses hesitated at this point, but I'm confident he must have at least paused!

So Moses reached out and grabbed it, and it turned back into a shepherd's staff in his hand.[11]

What shifted? Was it Moses' view of the stick? Of his own abilities? Or was it Moses' view of the one true living God?

We need a mindset shift regarding our belief in God's purpose and our part in his plan. For that to happen, I invite you to follow Moses' lead and release whatever mindset you might be holding onto about missions.

Let go of the notion that missions is only for a select, super-spiritual few.

Let go of the view that missions is outdated and irrelevant.

Let go of the concept of missions as merely a project that solves problems in the world.

Let go of the feeling that God can't use you.

Let go of the thought that missions is a department of the church.

Let go of the opinion that your church is too small, too new, too old, or too set in its ways to participate in missions.

Let go of the belief that you're too young or too old.

Let go of the myth that you can't afford it.

Let go of the idea that it's someone else's responsibility.

Let go of the impulse to hold too tightly to anything and everything that leads you to dismiss yourself or your church from this critical role in the mission of God.

As you release these things, I challenge you to remain empty-handed before God in a posture of surrender. As Romans 12:2 says, "Let God transform you into a new person by changing the way you think." I pray that, like Moses, you experience a mindset change concerning God and how he desires to use you in what he's doing in the world. God's mission is critical, and you have a meaningful and crucial part to play.

Jesus Started It

If the idea that you are commissioned feels daunting to you, keep in mind that you cannot mess up the story of what God is doing in the world. But you can miss out on your part in it! Stop waiting for a program or for permission. You can begin right now to reposition your heart and adjust your life. You are already doing meaningful things. But are you doing what matters most?

Dawson Trotman, founder of the Navigators, was passionate about discipleship. In a talk he gave in 1955, he said:

> Christians do important jobs, but not the most
> important. In every Christian audience, I am sure there
> are men and women who have been Christians for five,
> ten or twenty years but who do not know of one person
> who is living for Jesus Christ today because of them. I am
> not talking about merely working for Christ, but about
> producing for Christ.[12]

You were created by God, called to follow Christ, and commissioned to produce disciples. When Jesus gave this commission, it wasn't a last-minute thought before he ascended into heaven. It was a mandate for all followers to participate in a mission that was already in motion.

As Jesus commissioned his disciples, the mood on the mountain was mixed. The apostle Matthew writes, "When they saw him, they worshiped him—but some of them doubted!"[13] Yet, Jesus' mandate to "go and make disciples of all the nations"[14] was not a new idea. From the beginning, Jesus invited the disciples to participate in his mission, saying, "Come, follow me, and I will show you how to fish for people!"[15] They were called for this. They were trained for this.

You, too, are made for this! You are commissioned as an ambassador with a message for all people and given authority to speak on behalf of the King.[16]

In this book, you'll acquire the same necessary tools the disciples received from Jesus as he led them through an immersive experience of building the Kingdom. They gained knowledge, but they also learned the rhythm of tenacious obedience needed to participate in the most significant movement the world has ever known—a movement that is still happening today.

You'll Need an Open Bible and an Open Map

As you read further, you'll likely begin asking questions such as, "What is God's will for my life?" or "Where does my life fit into God's purpose?" Consider this quote that is widely attributed to a trailblazing missionary named William Carey: "To know the will of God, we need an open Bible and an open map."[17] In this book, we will open both.

You'll expand your missional view of the Bible and your biblical view of the world.

You'll increase your knowledge of nations and peoples and grasp the urgency of taking the gospel to the least-reached places on the earth.

You'll traverse the globe as we consider some global facts.

You'll pull up a chair to hear the stories of a great cloud of witnesses, both past and present, and gain perspective on how God *has* worked and *is* working for the sake of his name.

You'll be challenged to lead your church in disciple-making endeavors that do not shortcut the Great Commission by aiming at anything less than proclaiming the gospel to the ends of the earth.

For Every Follower of Christ

The Great Commission isn't for a select few but for every follower of Christ. Every word of this book was written with you in mind. My aim is not to convince you to uproot and move overseas—though you may. My aim is not for you to overhaul the ministries of your church—though you might. Instead, I hope to convince you of the truth that God's mission involves every believer (including you), and to encourage you to leverage every season of your life to advance the Kingdom of God.

My prayer is that what you read will kindle a desire in you to disrupt the status quo of faith in your life and within the church. When you know there is more to the Christian life than just showing up at church every Sunday, you will no longer be content with any discipleship that falls short of reaching more lives for Christ in every part of the world.

God's mission matters. Though I write from my experience of living overseas for a short time, partnering with missionaries and indigenous workers in more than thirty countries, working at a large missions-sending organization, and joining my husband in planting a missions-minded church, I am not an expert. My love for theology, missiology, and leadership drove me to pursue a seminary degree, but that degree simply etched deeper into my heart the need to continue learning and to integrate what I've learned into my own life as I lead, teach, and exhort others. At my core, I'm a practitioner. In my heart, I'm a catalyst. In my mind, I'm still learning.

Let's sojourn together. We are not a select few, but part of an army of Christ followers, summoned by the King and commissioned by his authority to advance his global cause. The Great Commission is not gender specific. We need both men's and women's voices to speak into critical, theological, missiological, and gospel-urgent matters. We need every believer to understand and celebrate how God has used and will continue to use all his sons and daughters to make disciples, lead in the church, and advance his Kingdom.

Is it too lofty a goal to desire that at the end of my life, and at the end of yours, we can say to God as Christ did, "I brought glory to you here on earth by completing the work you gave me to do"?[18]

As I write, my heart for you deeply echoes the words of the apostle Paul: "I plead with you, encourage you, and urge you to live your lives in a way that God would consider worthy. For he called you to share in his Kingdom and glory."[19]

Immeasurable:
The Ultimate Aim of God

*Life is the tale of two stories, one tiny and frail, the other eternal
and enduring. The tiny one, the story of us, is as brief as the blink
of an eye. Yet somehow our infatuation with our own little story—
and our determination to make it as big as we possibly can—blinds
us to the massive God Story that surrounds us on every side.*

LOUIE GIGLIO

PURPOSE. MEANING. SIGNIFICANCE.

We crave them and attempt to create them. Our hearts chase
them, and our minds dream about them. They move us, elude
us, seduce us, and deceive us. At times we think we have grasped
them, only to find they've slipped through our fingers.

Humanity ceaselessly strives to find purpose without considering what pastor Louie Giglio describes as the "massive God Story
that surrounds us on every side." Like attempting to assemble a
1,000-piece puzzle without ever looking at the image on the box,
we maneuver the pieces strewn about the table of life, wondering
if this piece fits here or that piece fits there. In times of frustration,
we might even force parts together, convincing ourselves that the
fit is close enough.

Not once have I attempted to assemble a puzzle without doing three things—looking at the picture on the box, gathering the straight-edged pieces to build the frame, and looking at the image on the box again, and again, and again.

It has been said, "The two most important days of your life are the day you were born and the day you find out why."[1] You know when you were born, but do you know why? To find the answer, many people try journaling, life coaching, or counseling. Though there's nothing wrong with those things—I've done them all—they won't help you discover why you exist and how you fit within the larger picture of God's mission.

We often approach the Bible as a self-help book filled with motivational taglines for life, but it's so much more. Like the straight-edged pieces of a puzzle, it frames thousands of interlocking pieces that form a comprehensive picture of who God is, what he's doing in the world, and why we exist. The puzzling part (pun intended) is that we are often uncertain about our piece of the puzzle.

We ask, "What is God's will for my life?" But the first question we need to ask is, "What is God's will for God?" In other words, the answer to this question functions something like the picture on the front of a puzzle box. As we look at that bigger picture, we'll discover that God's vision for our lives is better than any we could dream up on our own.

Let's take a closer look at the front of the box and allow God to align our hearts and our lives to the purpose for which he created us.

Discover God's purpose, and you'll find your own.

Identify Your Aim

In the 1960 NFL championship game, the Green Bay Packers blew a fourth-quarter lead and lost to the Philadelphia Eagles. When the next season began, Coach Vince Lombardi didn't present an innovative new playbook. Instead, he went back to basics. He entered the locker room at the first practice, held up an oblong pigskin filled with air, and said to his players, "Men, this is a football." He wasn't trying to insult their intelligence or minimize their experience, but to realign their thinking, simplify the task, and clarify their purpose.

Some of us have championed the church and been "professional Christians" for a long time. When we hear familiar words such as *missions*, *glory*, *discipleship*, and *the Great Commission*, we're so familiar with the terms that the fullness of their meaning ricochets off our hearts. So it's time to take a play from Coach Lombardi and get back to the basics. We need to realign our thinking, simplify our tasks, and clarify our purpose. I say *our* because that statement includes me. After thirty-one years of leading in ministry, I confess that it's too easy even for those of us in Christian leadership to lose sight of the goal. A continual flurry of projects, plans, programs, and problems diverts our attention and muddles our vision.

We invest time and waste time all at the same time.

We do important things, but not that which matters most.

We forget that which we are saved *from* and are prone to overlook that which we are saved *for*.

No matter how long you've been a Christian, consider this: If you could choose one phrase to sum up the direction of your life, what would it be? (We need to know what we're aiming at in order to tell if we're on course.)

Let's Begin at the End

Spoiler alert: We are starting at the end. Not at the end of the book, but at the end of your life, the end of the church, the completion of all history.

Sometimes, knowing the ending of a story makes us enjoy the story more. Perhaps that's why after telling a story to children, their immediate response is, "Tell it again!" Psychologists call this the "spoiler paradox," because knowing the end of the story doesn't diminish our enjoyment. In fact, researchers found that knowing the ending helps us do three things: simplify a complex story, process critical information, and understand a profound meaning.[2]

In the last book of the Bible, Revelation, God pulls back the curtain on eternity and allows us to peek inside as our imaginations travel to a time that does not yet exist but is certain to come. If you read Revelation and find yourself perplexed, congratulations! You are among the ranks of theologians who have studied it and feel the same way. One theologian used a phrase from Winston Churchill to describe the book: "If ever there was a book that could be described as 'a riddle, wrapped in a mystery, inside an enigma,' it is the last book in the Bible, the book of Revelation."[3]

Revelation, which means "to make known," wasn't written to keep us sidelined in controversial end-times conversations, but to activate us to obedience as we participate with God to accomplish his end aim—all nations worshiping him.

End Aim 1: Salvation Is Global Because God Is a Missionary God

Cue the cymbals and the drumroll. The Great Commission is concluded, the church's task is complete, and God's mission on earth ends. This is the climax of history, when both those who received him and those who rejected him will bow before him and "declare that Jesus Christ is Lord, to the glory of God the Father."[4]

Imagine you're standing before Christ's throne, surrounded by "a vast crowd, too great to count, from *every nation*."[5] Symphonic worship permeates the air when it's broadcast that Jesus is the only one able to open a sealed scroll because his "blood has ransomed people for God *from every tribe and language and people and nation.*"[6]

When you read "every nation" in Scripture, don't limit its meaning to geopolitical lines on a map that shape nearly two hundred countries. Governments are shaken, geographical boundaries shift, and names of countries change over time. The Greek words used for "nations" (*ethnē*) or "all nations" (*panta ta ethnē*) throughout the New Testament might be better understood as clusters of common cultures, rather than what we view as countries today.

This is epic! Salvation isn't just personal—it's global! And it flows out of the missionary character of God.

God is a missionary God whose limitless love for his creation generates a relentless pursuit of his creation. Bible scholars Andreas Köstenberger and Peter O'Brien put it this way: "The Lord of the Scriptures is a missionary God who reaches out to the lost, and sends his servants, and particularly his beloved Son, to achieve his gracious purposes of salvation."[7]

End Aim 2: Worship Is Inevitable and the Ultimate Aim of God

Global salvation is epic, but it's not ultimate. Eighteenth-century theologian Jonathan Edwards brilliantly said, "The great and last end of God's works . . . is indeed but *one*; and this *one* end is most properly and comprehensively called, THE GLORY OF GOD."[8]

God's glory is ultimate. It existed before Creation, exists in creation, and summons a Kingdom of worshipers in the new creation. It is the supreme end aim, the picture on the front of the puzzle box.

In eternity, there will be no sun or moon for God's glory will illumine the city.[9]

In eternity, all nations will worship before God.[10]

In eternity, "All mission has come to an end, and it becomes clear that mission is in fact a means to an end, the end being a *total focus* on the worship and the glory of God in our Lord Jesus Christ."[11]

It will require eternity and humanity in all its diversity to give the full measure of worship that the weight of God's glory deserves. A kaleidoscope of people will forever worship in linguistic harmony saying, "Worthy are you, our Lord and God, to receive glory and honor and power, for you created all things, and by your will they existed and were created."[12]

Salvation is global, worship is inevitable, eternity is inescapable, and God's glory is immeasurable.

God's glory is eternal, but God's mission is not.

God's glory will always be, but God's mission will end!

God Reveals His Glory to Receive Glory

A group of Muslim women entered the refugee center where I was working. Burkas covered their heads, and the traumatic experiences they'd endured covered their hearts. They gathered for simple needs—food, diapers, charging their phones, and friendship.

They sought meaning behind their experiences and were very open to hearing what the Bible had to say. With each passage of Scripture we shared, they drew a picture—for Creation, they drew a globe; for sin, they drew a broken heart. Once we got to Jesus, they drew a cross and a tomb. That's when one Iranian woman suddenly stopped drawing.

Knowing that Muslims believe Jesus was a prophet but not God's Son, and the Quran teaches that a man wrongly perceived to be Jesus hung on the cross,[13] I assumed that we hit an impasse.

"Why did you stop?" I asked.

She smiled and replied, "God cannot be contained to a piece of paper. He's much too big."

"This is very true," I said.

God is beyond our full understanding. At times we even question what in the world he's doing. The answer is this: He is making his name and glory known throughout the whole world. That's what he's about.

God Makes His Glory Known through His Creation

We cannot downsize God into an easily explained, user-friendly version. Doing so would be like trying to count the grains of sand on earth's 372,000 miles of seashore, trying to describe each rock that makes up the 229,731 square miles of the Himalayas, or trying to explain how light travels around the earth seven times in one second. Attempt any of these and you'll find yourself echoing Job's words: "I was talking about things I knew nothing about, things far too wonderful for me."[14]

Intrinsic is a word theologians use to describe God's glory.

Astronomers also use this word to define the *absolute* brightness of a star. Billions of stars fill the sky, many of them larger than the sun and millions of times farther away. Our eyes see only the *apparent* brightness of a star. Its *intrinsic* brightness, or how bright it really is, cannot be seen with the human eye.

God doesn't create his glory. It's who he is. He partially displays his intrinsic glory in what he creates. "For ever since the world was created, people have seen the earth and sky. Through everything God made, they can clearly see his invisible qualities—his eternal power and divine nature. So they have no excuse for not knowing God."[15]

God's glory is immeasurable. It is too large to be quantified or contained. King Solomon built a Temple for God and wrote, "Will

God really live on earth? Why, even the highest heavens cannot contain you. How much less this Temple I have built!"[16]

God displays his glory through his creation because he desires to be known and worshiped by his creation.

God Makes His Glory Known to His Creation

Just as an artist paints a portrait to reflect the image of a person, we were created to reflect the image of our Creator. We are the *imago Dei*, the image of God, created for God's glory and delight. The psalmist declares, "When you give them your breath, life is created. . . . The Lord takes pleasure in all he has made!"[17]

God delights in making himself known to his creation. As we come to understand the fullness of his delight in us, we desire to know and delight in him. As we delight in knowing him, we glorify him. As we glorify him, he delights in us. The more we experience his delight, the more we desire to glorify him.

And so it goes.

This is not a riddle. It's a relationship.

It is the reason for our existence. In the words of the Westminster Shorter Catechism: "Man's chief end is to glorify God, and to enjoy him forever." In doing so, we find that our life's joy and satisfaction are tethered to God's glory and his goodness.

God Receives Glory from His Creation

Look around. Everything created exalts the Creator!

The doxology in Psalm 148 elicits praise from creation under the branches of angelology, astronomy, zoology, marine biology, meteorology, botany, and ornithology, before it ever gets to humans. The psalmist invites everything God created to praise the Lord—the heavens, skies, angels, sun, moon, stars, clouds, vapors, ocean creatures, fire, hail, snow, wind, mountains, hills, trees, wild animals, livestock, birds, and—this one makes me laugh—scurrying animals. Then comes the finale, when the psalmist invites kings, rulers, judges, young men, young women, old men, and children to "Praise the LORD!"

All creation displays and declares God's glory. Yet we still find it difficult to describe God's glory without it sounding like a riddle.

God's glory is grand, yet its grandeur is inscrutable.
God's glory is majestic, yet its majesty is incomprehensible.
God's glory is made known to us, but it is unsearchable.

On this side of eternity, we will never fully comprehend God's glory. God makes his glory known to us so we can give glory to him. He has crowned us with his glory, and yet our sin separates us from his glory.

The Making of God's Mission

"You won't die!"[18] In a split moment, these deceptive words burrowed into the hearts of the serpent's two listeners. Satan twisted God's truth, dangled it in front of Adam and Eve, and they bit the bait—literally. They dismissed God's good design and desired to make their life as big as they could dream.

They could be like God!

They could have glory for themselves.

Glory isn't a word we often use to describe what drives our passions in life; instead, we tend to cloak our desire for glory in other ways. When our middle child was younger, he disguised his dream of becoming great as a passion for innovative thinking. He continually searched for the thing he could invent or discover. First, it was a solar-powered car, until he realized someone had already invented that technology. Then, it was the desalination of ocean water, yet someone had already blazed that trail as well. In his final attempt, he exclaimed, "I'll be the first to summit the highest mountain in the world!" As parents, we hated to crush his spirit, but we helped him research the story of Sir Edmund Hillary summiting Mount Everest in 1953.

He slumped in frustration and declared, "Well, there goes all my glory!" And there it was. His goal revealed. He wasn't passionate about the environment, clean water, or mountain climbing. His ten-year-old heart desired fame, renown, and glory.

Creation and God's mission both unfold in the first three chapters of Genesis.

Adam and Eve's rebellion resulted in utter destruction. Their life trajectory changed—and with it, the trajectory of all humanity. The *imago Dei* (image of God) needs the *missio Dei* (mission of God), or literally, "the sending of God."

God met the sin of Adam and Eve with condemnation, but also with a swift proclamation of future salvation. Their curse was laced with what theologians call the "first gospel" (from the Latin *protoevangelium* = *proto* ["first"] + *evangel* ["good news" or "gospel"]). In other words, the announcement of condemnation contained a message of future redemption.

God made two key promises in Genesis 3:15: (1) Satan would wound the offspring of the woman; but (2) this offspring (the Messiah) would ultimately crush Satan. The ruler of creation would redeem his creation for his own renown and glory.

Aim Small, Miss Small

In this chapter, I long to capture a glimmer of God's glory. For if the greatness of God never causes us to inhale his majesty, we will never move our feet to exhale his message. Theologian Keith

Whitfield puts it this way: "We will not be able to recover a vision and passion for missions until we recover the grandeur that God made us to know and worship him and to make him known throughout the whole earth."[19]

God's revelation of himself to us isn't only an invitation to know him but to join him in making him known. God revealed his glory to Isaiah as seraphim exclaimed, "Holy, holy, holy is the LORD of Heaven's Armies! The whole earth is filled with his glory!"[20]

Experiencing God caused Isaiah to recognize the extent of his sinfulness, to which he responded, "It's all over! I am doomed, for I am a sinful man."[21] After forgiving Isaiah, the Lord issued an invitation in the form of a question: "Whom should I send as a messenger to this people? Who will go for us?" And Isaiah demonstrated his willingness to make God known, saying, "Here I am. Send me."[22]

God is filling the earth with his glory, and he invites his creation to join in his global mission. When we align our lives with what God is aiming at, we will declare with Isaiah, "Your name and renown are the desire of our hearts."[23]

Benjamin Martin, a character played by Mel Gibson in the movie *The Patriot*, rallied two of his young sons to ambush British soldiers in revenge of his son's death. Hiding behind the camouflage of trees, he said, "Boys, do you remember what I taught you?" Shaking with fear, they held their rifles and replied, "Aim small, miss small." In other words, if we aren't aiming at the bull's-eye, we're apt to miss the target altogether. God's glory in all the earth is the epicenter at which we're to aim. Why? Because God's glory in all the earth is God's ultimate aim.

God's mission of making his glory known to all nations shouldn't be a footnote at the end of a church's vision statement.

It *is* the vision statement. God's mission defines not only the lives of those who live cross-culturally, but also the daily life of every Christ follower.

Since this is our aim, let us assess rightly how well our churches and our lives align with it. Are we leading our churches and making disciples to see God's glory realized in all the earth? Or are we aiming at peripheral activities and ministries that generate busyness but miss the target?

Let's realign with God's Word, his love for the world, and the global work he is doing for his glory.

2

Biblical: God's Mandate in All Scripture

The whole Bible is itself a "missional" phenomenon. The writings that now comprise our Bible are themselves the product of and witness to the ultimate mission of God.

CHRISTOPHER WRIGHT

ARISTOTLE SAID, "The soul never thinks without a picture." Let's test that idea.

I'll give you a word. When you read the word, notice the image that comes to mind.

Are you ready?

Here's the word: *house.*

What image comes to mind? A brick house? A mud hut? The White House? A dollhouse? Is it on a farm? In a slum? In a tree?

Now let's try it again with this word: *missions.*

What image comes to mind?

When I ask people this question, the number one thing they say is "Africa." Is that what came to mind for you too? Or was it orphans? The *JESUS* film? Did you imagine a remote village? An urban neighborhood?

Are *you* part of the picture?

Tucked away in our brains, we all have an image of what we think missions is. Let me invite you to access that image and allow God to edit your definition of his mission. Because what you believe about missions will determine how you behave.

When it comes to missions, many people think it is something that the spiritually elite do in far-off places. So, they dismiss themselves altogether from responsibility for missions. Or for some, missions is limited to a two-week overseas trip; when they return, their missions-focused behavior ends. Some churches focus on missions once a year during a special emphasis, but for the remaining fifty-one weeks of the year, missions is all but forgotten.

What if we have inadvertently distanced ourselves from participating in God's plan for his glory in all the earth because of a misconception about missions and our role in it?

It is essential for every believer and every church to understand that participating in God's mission is less about activities we do and more about joining God in what he's already doing. As pastor Jedidiah Coppenger writes, "It is difficult to talk about the *mission of God* without people thinking we are talking about *missions for God*. Of course, the difference between *missions* and *mission* is significant. The former is an activity of the church, and the latter is why we have a church."[1]

In other words, *missions* involves activities, but God's *mission* is why the church exists. As a disciple, you're a part of the church and therefore part of God's mission of making his name and glory known worldwide. If you've never considered that you have a role to play in God's mission, I understand. It wasn't until twenty years after I became a follower of Christ that I understood that *every* follower has a unique role to play.

Don't Dismiss Yourself Too Quickly

In the 1990s, my husband went on a missions trip to Kyiv, Ukraine. Communism had just crumbled, and borders opened, making the gospel accessible to those who once lived under government oppression. He returned telling stories of people hearing the gospel for the first time and eagerly following Jesus.

"I can't stay here and pastor at the same church and preach to the same people who have heard the same message when there are many who haven't heard it once," he said. Tears flooded his eyes, and his next words fell on my heart like a rock. "I think God is leading our family to move overseas as missionaries."

My mouth dropped. I held our three-month-old tight. I didn't say it, but I thought, *You'll get over it. Let's unpack your bags, put away the suitcases, and you'll come back to normal.*

Someone please tell me where we get the idea that there is such a thing as "normal Christianity"? There's nothing "normal" about following Christ. What we really mean is, "God, don't ask me to do anything uncomfortable."

We attend church, sing, pray, shake hands, and go home. Wash. Rinse. Repeat.

I was active in church. I was even in ministry. But missions wasn't on my radar.

I wasn't great at sharing the gospel. In hindsight, that wasn't the problem. The problem was that I had dismissed myself from having any role to play in God's mission here, there, or anywhere.

Nothing makes you search the Scriptures more than when you're perplexed. God began to open my eyes to see that the biblical narrative wasn't about me, as in, "God save me, help me, fix me, give me." The Bible is the revelation of God and his will. And he invites us to participate in his work in the world.

It Was Written

Jesus' mission wasn't a mystery. He told the disciples up front, "Come, follow me, and I will show you how to fish for people!"[2] But they didn't comprehend this any more than a lost American receiving directions in British-English. "Drive ten kilometers down the tarmac. After the flyover, give way at the roundabout and you'll see the petrol station on the right. Cheers." It's English, but unless you understand the vocabulary, its meaning is not obvious!

Jesus made his mission obvious.

Before he ascended into heaven, Jesus hosted a small group Bible study in which he basically went through the Old Testament. Don't yawn. Jesus repeatedly told religious people, "Your mistake is that you don't know the Scriptures," by which he meant the books we collectively refer to today as the Old Testament.[3]

The disciples needed to know that they were part of something written long ago. Jesus explained,

> "I told you that everything *written* about me in the law
> of Moses and the prophets and in the Psalms must be
> fulfilled." Then he opened their minds to understand the
> Scriptures. And he said, "Yes, it was *written* long ago that
> the Messiah would suffer and die and rise from the dead on
> the third day. It was also *written* that this message would
> be proclaimed in the *authority of his name to all the nations*,
> beginning in Jerusalem: 'There is forgiveness of sins for all
> who repent.' You are witnesses of all these things."[4]

In other words, you're part of something bigger than you! This mission is already in motion.

It's not new. It's biblical.

It's not yours. It's God's.

When we think of missions, we often go to the Great Commission verses. But God's global mission isn't segmented into a few choice New Testament verses that we print on matching missions trip T-shirts or stencil on the wall of the church foyer. The entire Bible is saturated with the mission of God. And it was the Old Testament that Jesus used to open the minds of the disciples to see his mission. He used Scripture they already knew to point them to a mission they didn't yet completely understand.

You Know Pieces. Do You Know the Point?

Perhaps the disciples could have told Sunday-school-sound-bite versions of Old Testament stories, as many of us can. God made a covenant with Abraham. But why? God sent ten plagues. But why? David killed Goliath. But why?

Do you know why? Complete this verse. "Be still and know that _____." Likely, you've read this Scripture. Sometimes it's shortened to *Be Still*, then printed on a pillow and sold online. You know a piece of this verse, but do you know the point? "Be still, and know that I am God! *I will be honored by every nation. I will be honored throughout the world.*"[5] This verse isn't about you and relaxation, it's about God and his exaltation in all the earth.

God's mission is stamped on the pages of the New Testament *and* the Old Testament. Theologian Christopher Wright states, "The God who walks the paths of history through the pages of the Bible pins a mission statement to every signpost on the way."[6]

Though I'm not going to dissect every Scripture verse or give much commentary, I want you to see how all the pieces of God's global activity fit together in chronological order and form a mission story already in motion.

Just as Jesus did with his disciples, let's follow a few of the Old Testament signposts recorded in the Law of Moses, the Prophets, and the Psalms that point us to the mission of God.

What follows is a list of eight categories that direct us to understand one unified mission theme.[7] In each category, we will answer "why" questions to help us weave together the big picture of God's mission. Don't just take it from me that you're a part of God's mission. I want you to see it in the same Old Testament Scriptures Jesus taught to his disciples.[8]

Creation
WHY DID GOD CREATE HUMANKIND?

You are precious to me. . . . I have made [you] *for my glory.*
ISAIAH 43:4,7

God blessed them. And God said to them, "Be fruitful and *multiply and fill the earth.*"
GENESIS 1:28, ESV

Have you ever asked yourself, *Why do I exist?* You are not an afterthought; you were created for God's glory. He designed his creation to multiply and fill the earth with his glory. "For the earth will be filled with the knowledge of the glory of the LORD as the waters cover the sea."[9]

Crisis
WHAT WAS THE RESULT OF SIN?

The LORD saw how great the *wickedness of the human race had become on the earth.* . . . The LORD regretted that he had made human beings on the earth.
GENESIS 6:5-6, NIV

God sent a flood to destroy everything but saved Noah and his family. When the waters subsided, God told Noah's family to "*multiply and fill the earth.*"[10]

HOW DID NATIONS COME TO BE?

> Now the whole world had one language. . . . Then they said, "Come, let us build ourselves a city, with a tower that reaches to the heavens, *so that we may make a name for ourselves; otherwise we will be scattered over the face of the whole earth.*" . . . The LORD confused the language of the whole world. From there *the Lord scattered them over the face of the whole earth.*
>
> GENESIS 11:1, 4, 9, NIV

HOW'S IT GOING SO FAR?

The events recorded in the first eleven chapters of Genesis span two thousand years. How is humanity doing?

God continually said: "Multiply and fill the earth."

Humanity said: "We don't want to fill the earth."

God said: "This is about my name and glory."

Humanity said: "We want to make a name for ourselves."

Covenant

WHY DID GOD BLESS ABRAHAM?

Finally, a turning point! The goal of God's glory didn't change, but God's approach shifted.

> *I will* make you into a *great nation*, and *I will* bless you; *I will make your name great*, and *you will* be a blessing. . . . And *all peoples on earth will be blessed through you.*
>
> GENESIS 12:2-3, NIV

WHY DID GOD BLESS ISAAC?

Through your descendants *all the nations of the earth* will be blessed.

GENESIS 26:4

WHY DID GOD BLESS JACOB?

All the families of the earth will be blessed through you and your descendants.

GENESIS 28:14

God blessed a few for the purpose of many. Or in Christopher Wright's words, "One nation is chosen, but all nations are to be the beneficiaries of that choice."[11]

Captivity, Calling Out, and Commandments

WHY DID GOD RAISE UP PHARAOH?

My great glory will be displayed through Pharaoh. . . . When *my glory* is displayed through them, all Egypt will *see my glory and know that I am the LORD!*

EXODUS 14:17-18

WHY DID GOD PART THE RED SEA?

Where is the one whose power was displayed when Moses lifted up his hand—the one who divided the sea before them, *making himself famous forever?*

ISAIAH 63:12

WHY DID GOD REDEEM HIS PEOPLE?

What other nation, O God, have you redeemed from slavery to be your own people? *You made a great name for yourself when you redeemed your people* from Egypt.

2 SAMUEL 7:23

WHY DID GOD SPARE THE ISRAELITES IN THE WILDERNESS?

I held back in order to protect *the honor of my name before the nations* who had seen my power in bringing Israel out of Egypt.

EZEKIEL 20:14

WHY DID GOD GIVE THE TEN COMMANDMENTS?

Obey them completely, and you will display your wisdom and intelligence *among the surrounding nations.*

DEUTERONOMY 4:6

God in his sovereignty is at work in humanity, and his activity demonstrates his glory. He uses pagan kings, plagues, people in captivity, and seas for his fame, his name, his honor, and his glory.

Conquest

God's reputation went before the Israelites as they crossed into the Promised Land. Rahab told the spies, "For we have heard how the LORD made a dry path for you through the Red Sea. . . . For the LORD your God is the supreme God of the heavens above and the earth below."[12] The surrounding nations worshiped tribal deities and idols. God made himself known by displaying his power through his people, Israel.

WHY DID GOD DRY UP THE WATERS CROSSING INTO THE PROMISED LAND?

For the LORD your God dried up the river right before your eyes. . . . *He did this so all the nations of the earth might know that the LORD's hand is powerful.*

JOSHUA 4:23-24

Kingdom

WHY DID DAVID KILL GOLIATH?

> I will kill you and cut off your head. . . . *And the whole world will know that there is a God* in Israel!
>
> 1 SAMUEL 17:46

WHY DID DAVID PRAY FOR BLESSING?

> May God be gracious to us and bless us and make his face shine on us—*so that your ways may be known on earth, your salvation among all nations.*
>
> PSALM 67:1-2, NIV

God is the ultimate King, and King David, who wrote many psalms, knew this. The book of Psalms reveals God's heart for the nations. It is filled with songs calling the nations to worship God and declare his glory in all the earth.

Kingdom Divided

Israel continually rebelled and the kingdom was divided. God's people were taken captive by the Assyrians; the Babylonians scattered them; and then the Persians allowed some to return home.

During this time, God sent prophets to speak his word to them.

WHAT WAS GOD'S PLAN DURING CAPTIVITY?

> I will also make you a light for the Gentiles, that *my salvation may reach to the ends of the earth.*
>
> ISAIAH 49:6, NIV

WHY DID GOD WITHHOLD HIS ANGER WHEN ISRAEL REBELLED?

> *For my name's sake* I defer my anger; *for the sake of my praise* I restrain it for you, that I may not cut you off. . . .

For my own sake, I do it, for how should *my name* be
profaned? *My glory I will not give to another.*

ISAIAH 48:9-11, ESV

Come Home and Construct

WHY DID GOD BRING ISRAEL OUT OF EXILE?

I am bringing you back, but not because you deserve it.
*I am doing it to protect my holy name. . . . Then the nations
will know* that I am the LORD.

EZEKIEL 36:22-23

WHY DID GOD USE NEHEMIAH TO REBUILD THE WALLS?

I will bring you back to the place I have chosen for my
name to be honored.

NEHEMIAH 1:9

It is this Old Testament story of God's purpose for all creation, his salvation for all nations, and his relentless pursuit of
worship from all peoples that provides the platform from which
Jesus gives his Great Commission.

The Old Testament was the theological foundation for the
disciples' understanding of the Great Commission, and it is the
theological foundation for us. God's mission from the beginning has been to make his name and glory known in all the
earth.

We're Part of a Much Bigger Story

When you talk about the Great Commission at church, do people
understand that it's connected to a much larger story? If you're a
teacher, a pastor, a small group leader, or a parent, do those you
influence know that they are part of a story bigger than themselves?

If people don't know the story that they are part of, how can they participate in it?

My hope is that the brief passages you read on the previous pages lead you to see that the entire Bible is one unified story about God's mission for his name and glory among all nations. I challenge you to take notice of phrases like "for the sake of my name," or "for my glory," or "among all nations" as you read through the Bible.

Not to oversimplify Scripture, or God's activity in all history, but if we take each chronological section above and put them visually together, where do you fit?

You are part of the story.

Look at the picture showing all the connections and find your location. Added in are Christ, the "radiance of God's glory";[13] the church, sent to declare God's glory; and finally, the new creation, where all nations worship God and bring him glory for all eternity.

Do you see yourself in the story?

Remember, *you cannot mess up the mission of God, but you can miss out on it.*

Jesus opened the disciples' eyes to see what we all need to see.

From the beginning of time, God has been working in the world for the sake of his name and glory among all nations.

God sent his Son, Jesus, who died and rose again.

Forgiveness of sins must be proclaimed in his name to all nations.

You are a witness to these things.

You are part of a significant story, but the story isn't about you.

Your contribution to the story is essential, but you're not the author.

Your role is important, but you're not the main character.

You have a purpose, but you're not the point.

God created you for it, but you're not the center of it.

The story is true, and it's still being written—and you have a part to play!

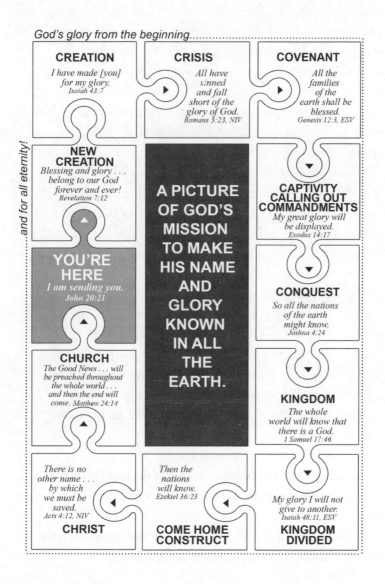

God's glory from the beginning..

...and for all eternity!

CREATION
I have made [you] for my glory.
Isaiah 43:7

CRISIS
All have sinned and fall short of the glory of God.
Romans 3:23, NIV

COVENANT
All the families of the earth shall be blessed.
Genesis 12:3, ESV

NEW CREATION
Blessing and glory . . . belong to our God forever and ever!
Revelation 7:12

CAPTIVITY CALLING OUT COMMANDMENTS
My great glory will be displayed.
Exodus 14:17

YOU'RE HERE
I am sending you.
John 20:21

A PICTURE OF GOD'S MISSION TO MAKE HIS NAME AND GLORY KNOWN IN ALL THE EARTH.

CONQUEST
So all the nations of the earth might know.
Joshua 4:24

CHURCH
The Good News . . . will be preached throughout the whole world . . . and then the end will come. Matthew 24:14

KINGDOM
The whole world will know that there is a God.
1 Samuel 17:46

There is no other name . . . by which we must be saved.
Acts 4:12, NIV
CHRIST

Then the nations will know.
Ezekiel 36:23
COME HOME CONSTRUCT

My glory I will not give to another.
Isaiah 48:11, ESV
KINGDOM DIVIDED

3

Critical: An Inclusive and Exclusive Gospel

Whereas disinfecting Christians involves isolating them and teaching them to be good, discipling Christians involves propelling Christians into the world to risk their lives for the sake of others.

DAVID PLATT

PICTURE A REMOTE VILLAGE. During the rainy season, the dirt roads are impassible even to the best of four-wheeled vehicles. But during the dry season, the ground is so hot the villagers say it's like "walking on fire." A large tree stands in the village with bone fragments from frogs and birds wrapped in maize husks and tied to its branches like ornaments.

Intrigued, I pulled out my camera, but then a local woman quickly grabbed my arm to stop me. "Taking a photo will steal the tree's spirit," she said, "and people who worship it will not be happy." Respectfully, I put my camera away.

Late that night, I sat around a campfire with people from the village who represented generations who prayed to this tree. They lived every day in fear of ancestral spirits. They tied fetishes in their hair and beaded strings around their children's waists to keep evil spirits away. In the glow of firelight, we sat exchanging stories about our lives. As we shared, I told stories from the Bible about a God who created all things—trees, birds, frogs, and people. He loved his creation and called it good. God loved people so much that he sent his only Son to die for them. God's Son defeated evil, so they would not have to live in fear. I could barely see their eyes, but I heard one woman clearly say, "We do not know who God's Son is."

Tension fills my heart every time I'm around someone who has *never* heard the name of Jesus. One side of my heart questions, "How in the world is this possible?" But the other side of my heart rejoices, "Let me introduce you to him!"

The Gospel Unleashed

Meet the Savior of the world! Or, in Philip's words, "We have found the very person Moses and the prophets wrote about! His name is Jesus."[1]

Jesus is the radiance of God's glory![2] And in his glory, he loves you, chooses you, came for you, died for you, saves you, forgives you, redeems you, restores you, and longs to spend eternity with you. This is amazing news!

"This is real love—not that we loved God, but that he loved us and sent his Son as a sacrifice to take away our sins."[3] There's no way to sugarcoat the sin that sent Jesus to the cross. Sin isn't simply a mistake, a slipup, or doing something stupid. Sin is treason. It's a rebellious uprising in our souls to revolt against the King and his authority.

No matter who we are or where we live, all of us have the same problem. We are all alienated from God, dead in our sin, living in discord with one another, utterly helpless, and condemned to eternity in hell. "Adam's sin brought death, so death spread to everyone, for everyone sinned."[4]

Death was your trajectory until you entrusted your life to God and experienced his "wonderful grace and his gift of forgiveness" through Jesus Christ.[5] Now that you have received the critical message of salvation, you possess critical information to lead others to salvation. As you celebrate your salvation, realize that he desires to bring salvation to the whole world. The gospel didn't come to you to end with you. It came *to you* through someone and is intended to go *through you* to someone else.

Following Christ is not a Monopoly game in which the goal is to accumulate biblical information, build bigger spiritual institutions, possess exclusive rights to the gospel, or hoard Jesus as if he's our personal get-out-of-hell-free card. As George Robinson puts it, "The gospel saves us from sin, for God, into the church, and onto his mission."[6] The gospel is unleashed and on the move through you to someone else.

An Inclusive and Exclusive Gospel

Every day as the sun rises in India, the ringing of bells breaks the morning silence. Hindus shake tambourines or small chimes to awake their gods for *puja* (prayer and worship).

One morning on the outskirts of a Hindu temple, I noticed a kiosk where figurines representing various gods could be purchased. Imagine going to a sports store with all your favorite teams' paraphernalia lining the walls. That's what this was, except the stand contained representations of some of the 330 million gods that Hindus pick and choose from.

Mixed in with Shiva, Ganesh, and other gods was a statue of Jesus. Pointing to Jesus and another god, I asked the storekeeper, "What's the difference between these two?"

"They are both good and lead to good things," he replied.

Hindus believe Jesus is *a* god but not *the* God.

Muslims believe Jesus was a prophet but not the Son of God.
Jews believe Jesus was a teacher but not the Messiah.
Buddhists believe Jesus was an enlightened holy man but not a giver of eternal life.

And 3.37 billion people have yet to hear of Jesus at all![7]

Our invitation to follow Christ is an invitation to further his Kingdom with the critical message of an inclusive and exclusive gospel. God loves everyone, and he provides a way of salvation available to everyone—but only *one* way.

For God so loved the world, that he gave his only Son,
that whoever believes in him should not perish but have
eternal life. For God did not send his Son into the world
to condemn the world, but in order that the world might
be saved through him.

JOHN 3:16-17, ESV

These verses affirm that the gospel is both *inclusive* and *exclusive*—it is an inclusive message for everyone, but with an exclusive message that Jesus is the only one who can save us.

Inclusive = God so loved *the world* that he gave his only Son.
Exclusive = Whoever believes *in him* will not perish but have eternal life.
Inclusive = Jesus did not come to condemn *the world.*
Exclusive = But in order that the world might be saved *through him.*

The gospel is both inclusive and exclusive.

Even with all our innovation, modernization, and invention, we cannot fix the human problem of sin and eternal condemnation.

We've mastered flight, walked on the moon, eradicated some diseases, and harnessed electricity, but we cannot orchestrate a way to restore humanity's severed relationship with God or fabricate a way to have eternal life. Jesus made it clear: "The Spirit alone gives eternal life. Human effort accomplishes nothing."[8]

All roads don't lead to heaven—though I've heard this idea from Muslims, Hindus, Buddhists, and those who claim no religion. I've even heard some who claim to be Christians say, "We're all just doing our best and hoping for good in the end."

Following Jesus liberates us from sin, but it doesn't give us the liberty to water down the truth to make it more palatable or tolerant. Jesus isn't one way among many options. He is *the* Way, the only way, and no one comes to God except through him.[9] All may come, but the gate is narrow and the road, difficult.[10]

Messy Discipleship

Although we have mentioned the Great Commission, we haven't yet unpacked the statement itself. That's because we first need to lay the foundation for the Great Commission by understanding three things:

- God's ultimate aim is his glory.
- God's mission is the thread connecting the stories in the Bible.
- Jesus calls his disciples to be close to him—before he commissions them.

Jesus did more than teach the disciples Scripture. He initiated a personal relationship with them, instigated learning opportunities, and for three years invited them into his everyday life.

Their training took time.

Every day they spent with Jesus was a messy discipleship lab. And it didn't take place within the contained walls of ministry and calendared events, but within the context of culture, community, and conversations. If they were going to be leaders in a movement, they needed to learn from the Master. If they were going to lead others in the cause of Christ, they first needed to learn to live like Jesus.

When Jesus ascended to heaven, his ministry on earth didn't fall apart; it multiplied—and the disciples were part of igniting the greatest movement in all history.

But first, they learned to seek him.

Then they learned to submit to him.

Ultimately, they were sent by him.

Don't miss the order. Jesus called the disciples to be close to him so he could commission them. We're apt to miss the purpose clause in Mark's fast-paced words, "And he appointed twelve (whom he also named apostles) *so that* they might be *with him* and he might *send them* out to preach."[11]

Here, the expression "so that" translates the Greek conjunction *hina*, which is often used to introduce a purpose clause. Sometimes a *hina* clause connotes both purpose and result, particularly when God is the subject, suggesting that what God wills is certain to happen. Jesus didn't appoint the apostles with simply the potential that they would go out, but with certainty that he would send them out to preach. It wasn't an optional call but a mission-critical one.

Jesus didn't need followers to know *about* him but to intimately know *him*. That's why after the apostles returned from their first solo missions and were celebrating their accomplishments, Jesus said, "Don't rejoice because evil spirits obey you; rejoice because your names are registered in heaven."[12] In other words, our identity *in* Jesus is more important than our activity *for* Jesus. He initiates and delights in intimate relationships with his followers and desires that they, too, delight in an intimate relationship with him.

Are you consuming God's Word and spending time in prayer? Take a moment to slow down and consider that question.

I'm not asking if you've checked a list this week, or if you've been doing church-related activities. I'm asking whether you've actively delighted in a reciprocal, intimate relationship with Christ in his Word and in prayer.

Jesus said, "Those who remain in me, and I in them, will produce much fruit. For apart from me you can do nothing. . . . When you produce much fruit, you are my true disciples. This brings great glory to my Father."[13] Remaining in a relationship means abiding in unceasing, God-glorifying intimacy. Our intimacy with Jesus produces not just *some* fruit, but *much* fruit. This is much more than going through a routine to manufacture fruit that looks spiritual.

Theologian David Bosch wrote, "Mission in the New Testament is more than a matter of obeying a command. It is, rather, the result of an encounter with Christ."[14] That's why those who know Christ intimately proclaim him confidently. Intimacy develops our ability to follow him, enlarges our capacity to produce fruit, and increases our tenacity to proclaim him.

Enlarged Heart and Expanded Worldview

The disciples had a lot to learn and a lot to unlearn. They were self-absorbed, ethnocentric, and nationalistic. Jesus dismantled their life plans, deconstructed their thought patterns, rerouted the paths they traveled, and disassembled the scaffolding propping up their religion.

We have a compelling example of Jesus doing this training work in the apostle John's account of Jesus and the Samaritan woman.[15] In the passage, John brilliantly combines two stories into one. We get a panoramic view of the gospel as Jesus presents it in conversation with the woman, and we get a peek at Jesus' hands-on, cross-cultural training with his disciples. Take a moment to read John 4:1-42 in your Bible, and then we'll take a closer look at the lessons Jesus invites his disciples to learn and unlearn. With each lesson, you'll have a chance to do a heart check to consider the lessons you might need to learn or unlearn as well.

Jesus Disrupted Their Predictable Path

Talk about culture shock! Jesus and his disciples were traveling from Judea to Galilee when Jesus intentionally ignored the usual route and took his students on a trip through Samaritan territory.

Jews, including the disciples, didn't have just a minor dislike of Samaritans; they harbored generations worth of disdain. So when the disciples returned from the town to find Jesus engaged in conversation with the Samaritan woman, the ethnocentric tension would have been thick and the disciples' prejudice palpable. We know how the story ends. The woman believed in Jesus and shared the Good News with others, and many in her village followed.

There was a reason that Jesus first chose to travel the unpredictable path from Judea to Galilee that took them through hostile Samaritan territory. Instead of simply telling the disciples to love people who were different, Jesus initiated an opportunity for hands-on learning. He modeled what it looked like to cross cultures, to have an authentic and meaningful engagement with those who were different from them.

Crossing cultures challenges every part of us. When God leads us to engage with people different from us, he's not just moving our feet—he's expanding our hearts.

HEART CHECK

How do you tend to respond when God interrupts your plans or challenges your prejudices?

When was the last time you went out of your way to engage in an intentional relationship with someone?

How willing are you to risk an unknown path, trusting that God is with you? Entirely willing, somewhat willing, unwilling? Why?

As you engage in gospel conversations or cross cultures, who are you taking with you so that they can learn from you?

Jesus Defied Cultural Norms for a Gospel Purpose

When the disciples left to buy food, Jesus stayed behind and had his one-on-one conversation with the Samaritan woman. In twenty verses, John shows us Jesus' gospel strategy.

1. He initiated a conversation: "Please give me a drink."[16]
2. He converted the conversation into a gospel opportunity: "If you only . . . would ask me, . . . I would give you living water."[17]
3. He took an interest in her personal life without condemning her: "Go and get your husband."[18]
4. He built a bridge of trust by talking about her religion: "The time is coming when it will no longer matter whether you worship the Father on this mountain or in Jerusalem."[19]
5. He introduced her to the Messiah: "I AM the Messiah!"[20]

The gospel conversation itself wasn't as straightforward as a list. Seven times the woman made a rebuttal or asked a question. But with patience, Jesus walked with her every step of the way.

HEART CHECK

How willing are you to go against cultural norms to share the gospel? Entirely willing, somewhat willing, or unwilling? Why?

In what ways, if any, do spiritual conversations intimidate you?

What experiences have you had of converting a conversation into a gospel opportunity? What happened? What did you learn as a result?

Jesus Challenged Their Worldview concerning What Matters Most

The disciples returned just as Jesus finished his conversation and the woman left. And this is where things get fun!

Jaws dropped and the disciples were speechless. None of them had the nerve to ask why he was breaking cultural norms by talking to a Samaritan woman. An awkward silence filled the air.

Finally, someone jumped in with the safest topic—food. When in doubt, talk about food!

When the disciples urged Jesus to eat something, his response is the hinge on which the entire story swings: "I have a kind of food you know nothing about. . . . My nourishment comes from doing the will of God, who sent me, and from finishing his work."[21]

Jesus allowed the disciples to be perplexed for a moment, and then he challenged their worldview. By *worldview*, I don't mean what the disciples thought about the world, but the lens through which they saw it.[22] He took their cultural lens and gave them a spiritual way to see. He said, "You know the saying, 'Four months between planting and harvest.' But I say, wake up and look around. The fields are already ripe for harvest."[23] And as they looked around, they could see the entire village walking toward them.

In Jesus' economy, we cannot calculate when the spiritual harvest will come. Jesus planted a seed in a woman's heart, it multiplied and grew with divine speed, and the disciples were part of reaping the harvest.

HEART CHECK

In what ways, if any, does this story challenge your worldview about what matters most?

If Jesus were to say to you, "Wake up and look around," what do you imagine you might see? What spiritual fields might be ripe for harvest?

If you believe God is on a mission to make his name known in all the earth, what might that mean for you? How do you understand your role in that mission?

Born to Reproduce

The disciples couldn't lead like Christ until they learned to live like Christ. And Jesus had to disrupt, counter, and challenge their worldview to make that possible. Like the disciples, we often need a dose of disequilibrium so that God can enlarge our hearts and expand our worldview.

All evidence points to the fact that those of us in the Western church are not reproducing disciples. Rather, we are creating environments in which people select, sit, study, and stay.

Dawson Trotman, founder of the Navigators, said,

Wherever you find a Christian who is not leading men and women to Christ, something is wrong. . . .

Men, where is your man? Women, where is your woman? Where is the one whom you led to Christ and who is now going on with Him? . . .

What will it take to jar us out of our complacency and send us home to pray, "God, give me [someone] whom I can win to Christ"? [24]

How would the people in your church answer these questions? How do you answer them?

A recent survey sponsored by Exponential, a church multiplication ministry, found that fewer than 5 percent of US churches "have a reproducing disciple-making culture."[25] However, some churches who reported making disciples offered no evidence of church growth or baptisms to support their claims. This suggests that our idea of discipleship isn't really producing disciples who reproduce other disciples.

My church has had to do some honest assessment of our discipleship efforts. I didn't realize it at the time, but I was incorrectly measuring the disciple-making culture of the ministry I led. Twice a year, I put together opportunities to join six-week Bible studies. People excitedly signed up, but two weeks in, attendance was hit-and-miss. Four weeks in, we lost some. Six weeks in, people were sitting in the parking lot hurriedly filling in the blanks in their workbooks right before start time.

During the off-season, usually the summer months, people often asked, "When's the next study?"

One day, I started asking back, "What are you doing now?"

The most common response was, "Nothing." People were hungry for God's Word, but they didn't know how to feed themselves, much less lead others to know Christ and study his Word.

Discipleship is more than signing up for a small-group Bible study. Disciples produce fruit. Jesus modeled messy discipleship. He initiated an intimate relationship with his disciples and often taught in small settings.

Pastor Kyle Idleman notes, "The Bible records Jesus speaking to crowds only fifteen times but having *forty* one-on-one conversations."[26] And it isn't often that we see Jesus teaching his disciples in a synagogue; instead, we see him teaching them through life experiences, such as when he led his disciples in the encounter with the Samaritan woman.

How would you characterize your relationships with other Christians? As you read through the contrasting descriptions below, consider which one best describes those relationships.

- Mentoring is a come-and-go relationship. Discipleship is a come-and-follow-me relationship.
- Bible studies are a join-my-group relationship. Discipleship is a join-my-life relationship.
- Preaching is a come-and-listen-to-me relationship. Discipleship is a come-and-imitate-me relationship.
- Church events are a let's-come-together relationship. Discipleship is a let's-go-out-together relationship.

We have a gospel that is both inclusive and exclusive. Salvation is for everyone, but Jesus is the only one through whom everyone can be saved. A decision to follow Christ is an invitation to be a disciple that produces other disciples. Pastor David Platt offers a helpful distinction between "disinfecting" Christians and discipling them:

[Instead of] just going, baptizing, and teaching, . . . we resist this plan, resorting to performances and programs that seem much more "successful." [But] our plan ends up disinfecting Christians *from* the world more than discipling Christians *in* the world. . . .

Whereas disinfecting Christians involves isolating them and teaching them to be good, discipling Christians involves propelling Christians into the world to risk their lives for the sake of others.[27]

Disciples and mission are not separated from one another but integrated. Discipleship is mission critical.

4

Possible: God's Mission Will Happen

We have been guilty of acting more like the beleaguered garrison of a doomed fortress than like soldiers of our ever-conquering Christ. . . . Shall we beat a retreat, and turn back from our high calling in Christ Jesus; or dare we advance at God's command, in face of the impossible?

JOHN C. STAM

"WE MUST BE BOLD."

The year was 1962, and President John F. Kennedy was determined to put a man on the moon. In an address at Rice University in Houston, he listed the criteria that must be met to achieve what seemed impossible:

> If I were to say, my fellow citizens, that we shall send to the moon, 240,000 miles away from the control station in Houston, a giant rocket more than 300 feet tall, the length of this football field, made of new metal alloys, some of which have not yet been invented, capable of standing heat and stresses several times more than have ever been experienced, fitted together with a precision better than the finest watch, carrying all the

equipment needed for propulsion, guidance, control, communications, food and survival, on an untried mission, to an unknown celestial body, and then return it safely to earth, re-entering the atmosphere at speeds of over 25,000 miles per hour, causing heat about half that of the temperature of the sun—almost as hot as it is here today—and do all this, and do it right, and do it first before this decade is out—then we must be bold.[1]

It was an "untried mission" that would cost "a staggering sum"—though, as Kennedy noted, the amount would be "somewhat less than we pay for cigarettes and cigars every year."[2]

The United States prioritized rallying a nation, exploring innovation, developing education, and training people for a task that had never before been attempted.

I wonder how many collective hours were spent inventing the necessary metals. I wonder how many citizens grumbled about having more of their tax dollars going to a program with no tangible benefit to their daily lives. I wonder how many anticipated the successful completion of the project and how many scoffed in disbelief. I wonder about the emotions of those who risked their lives to step into a rocket the size of a football field, fully aware they were being propelled into the unknown.

In presenting his case for the space mission, President Kennedy made it clear that it wouldn't be easy. It would require an intense, coordinated effort to put a man on the moon.

Achieving a bold mission isn't something individuals can do on their own, and Jesus knew this. When he issued his mandate to make disciples among all people groups of the world, Jesus knew it would require participation, contribution, and effort from everyone. There's no abbreviating it, delegating it, or wiggling out of it.

We must rally the church, activating and equipping people for an "untried mission."

It will cost us.

We must be bold.

It's not easy; it's hard.

But it is possible. Correction—it is more than possible.

It's inevitable.

It will happen. "The Good News about the Kingdom *will* be preached throughout the whole world, so that all nations *will* hear it; and then the end *will* come."[3] The question is, will you and your church join with joy in the effort?

The Great Commission(s) in the Gospels

The term *Great Commission* isn't in Scripture. Who originally coined the phrase to describe Jesus' final words prior to his ascension is a matter of speculation. Some believe it may have been William Carey, the eighteenth-century father of the modern missions movement. Others cite missionaries and pastors from as early as the sixteenth century.

Hudson Taylor, a nineteenth-century missionary to China, elevated the term when he wrote, "The Great Commission is not an option to be considered; it is a command to be obeyed."[4] Others argue it was not a command, but rather a mandate or commission. While a command gives instructions, such as "Do not steal" or "Walk the dog," a commission confers authority and responsibility to engage in something significant, something bigger than yourself.[5]

God sent Jesus. Jesus accomplished what he was sent to do.[6] Jesus appointed the apostles,[7] which means "sent-ones." When Jesus spoke the words we now refer to as the Great Commission, he wasn't just commissioning those present with him, but all who would ever follow him, including us. And we were on his mind even before he went to the cross. Jesus prayed, "I am praying not only for these disciples but also for all who will ever believe in me through their message."[8]

As a follower of Christ, you are commissioned.

Scholars believe the five passages documenting Jesus' commission—recorded in Matthew, Mark, Luke, John, and Acts—represent five separate occasions, rather than one occasion written five different ways. We'll explore the four accounts recorded in the Gospels in this chapter, and we'll consider the account recorded in Acts in the next chapter.

I Am Sending You

THE GREAT COMMISSION IN JOHN 20:21-22

The disciples met behind locked doors. You would, too, if your teacher had just been killed by the authorities and you were identified as a follower. Somehow, Jesus appeared in their midst. His message was short, sweet, and sobering. "'As the Father has sent me, so I am sending you.' Then he breathed on them and said, 'Receive the Holy Spirit.'"[9] I wonder if anyone remembered at that point that Jesus had previously told them he would send a helper and they would do even greater works than he had.[10]

Preach Repentance in Jesus' Name

THE GREAT COMMISSION IN LUKE 24:46-48

A couple of disciples had walked right beside the resurrected Christ on their way to Emmaus, and they hadn't even known who he was. After they recognized him, they told each other how their hearts had burned while he spoke with them. When they told the other disciples about their experience, Jesus suddenly appeared among them. Luke captures all the emotions they felt at one time—fear, doubt, joy, and wonder! Then Jesus, while eating fish, opened their eyes to understand the Scriptures.[11] He said,

It was written long ago that the Messiah would suffer and die and rise from the dead on the third day. It was also written that this message would be proclaimed in the authority of his name to all the nations, beginning in Jerusalem: "There is forgiveness of sins for all who repent." You are witnesses of all these things.[12]

The commission in Luke is a prediction that will come to fruition. Proclaiming forgiveness in Jesus' name will cause people from all nations to change their minds about God.[13] But they can't change their minds and repent unless they hear the message.

Preach the Good News
THE GREAT COMMISSION IN MARK 13:9-11; 16:9-16
Some earlier manuscripts don't include Mark's version of Christ's commission. Though it's not conclusive, there is evidence to suggest that Mark 16:9-16 is not the original ending to Mark's Gospel. Nevertheless, the verses demonstrate consistency concerning Jesus' message for all nations and his promise to send the Holy Spirit. Jesus' words during his earthly ministry align with his commission: "You will stand trial before governors and kings. . . . This will be your opportunity to tell them about me. For the Good News must first be preached to all nations. . . . For it is not you who will be speaking, but the Holy Spirit."[14]

Go and Make Disciples
THE GREAT COMMISSION IN MATTHEW 28:18-20
It is in Matthew's account that the disciples worship Jesus for the first time as the resurrected Savior of the world! However, Matthew also notes "but some of them doubted!"[15] Jesus didn't try to convince the doubters but instead commissioned them all.

Jesus knew what he would accomplish through them in the power of his Spirit. They just didn't know it yet. He said,

> I have been given all authority in heaven and on earth. Therefore, go and make disciples of all the nations, baptizing them in the name of the Father and the Son and the Holy Spirit. Teach these new disciples to obey all the commands I have given you. And be sure of this: I am with you always, even to the end of the age.[16]

How to Make Disciples

It has been said that last words are lasting words. Though Matthew 28:18-20 is most often cited when speaking about the Great Commission, in Jesus' final words before his ascension (Acts 1:8) he confirms the mandate to *go* and reveals that the power for evangelism will come from the Holy Spirit.

Jesus, with limitless power, gives a mandate with no expiration date to go and inundate the world with the gospel.

> The foundation of the commission is that Jesus has *all authority*.
> The location of the commission is *all nations*.
> The duration of the commission is *all days*.
> The instruction of the commission is to teach *all commands*.
> The inspiration of the commission is that he is with us *always*.

Make disciples is the main imperative verb in the commission. *Go*, *baptize*, and *teach* communicate how we make disciples.[17] Each component is essential to fulfilling the mission correctly.

Go

I didn't want to talk to anyone on the plane. I wanted to read. But the guy next to me was chatty. Not only that, but his thick

Hawaiian-Japanese accent forced me to watch his mouth to understand what he was saying. Exasperated, I closed my book, which had the word *Bible* in the title. After seeing it, he asked, "Are you a Christian?"

"I am," I said. "Are you?"

"Well, I've heard that I'm going to hell unless I convert to being a Baptist," he said.

I laughed on the inside. Before I could respond, he asked, "Are you a Baptist?"

"I'm a follower of Jesus," I said.

I was so consumed with my spiritual book that I nearly missed a spiritual opportunity. No, he didn't pray to become a follower during our flight. A lot of people with whom we share the gospel may not choose to follow Christ right then. But we are simply called to be obedient and share the gospel with them.

The Greek word translated *go* in Matthew 28:19 could convey the sense of "as you go." That has a nice ring to it, doesn't it? Simply make disciples wherever you happen to be. Live as a sent one wherever you are! Or, as Martin Luther said, "Toward my neighbor I will also become a Christ, as Christ became for me."[18]

Leverage your life, your job, or your airplane ride. Convert a conversation into a gospel opportunity at the gym, across the street, or in the restaurant. It requires eyes that look for the right moments, a heart willing to bend, feet ready to move, hands postured to help, ears inclined to listen, and a mouth eager to speak. In every way, share Jesus on your way. Implement the declaration of the psalmist, "All day long I will proclaim your saving power, though I am not skilled with words."[19]

But "as you go" is not just a casual stroll. If we limit obedience to the Great Commission to the convenience of wherever we happen to be in the moment, we've missed the point of God's mission and the entire biblical narrative.

The Greek participle translated *go* isn't temporal and casual. It's forceful. It takes on the mood of the main verb, *make disciples*. In other words, "Go! And, as you go, make disciples!"[20]

The interpretation isn't lackadaisical and local. It's global.

Yes, make disciples as you go, but also go out of your way to make disciples. Make disciples in the place you call home *and* be willing to relocate your home to a place where the gospel hasn't been. That means we cannot shrink the Great Commission to "make disciples" and bypass going to "all the nations." Discipleship without a vision for the nations is deficient at best and disobedient at worst.

Jesus' commission is a mandate to participate in the unfolding story of God's glory among all nations—or, more precisely, all ethnicities. This is where we are to make disciples. Remember how far back the continuous thread of God's mission goes? As far back as God's covenant with Abraham, we see God's intention to bless "all peoples on earth."[21] And remember where God's mission concludes? At the end of time when all peoples are gathered around Christ's throne.[22] The time we live in now is the in-between. It is the time to "go and make disciples of all the nations," the means and the method of gathering worshipers who will glorify God for eternity.

Baptize

Ali, a refugee from Afghanistan, fled to Greece, where he met a former Muslim who taught him about Jesus. Ali's joy in becoming a Christian was contagious. When the day came for him to be baptized, as we stood on the shore of the Aegean Sea, he looked at the phone in my hand, and with a mixture of broken English and hand motions asked me to take his photo when he came up from the water. "But," he added, "don't post to Facebook. My family will . . ." Then he used his finger to mimic someone slitting his throat.

Ali knew the profound meaning of baptism. He understood that his actions were a public declaration that he was a Jesus follower.

Baptism is an act of obedience that marks a "loyalty change."[23] No matter the language differences, baptism communicates the same visible message. It publicly declares our faith in Jesus Christ alone, symbolizing that we are united with Christ in his death, burial, and resurrection. We have "put on Christ, like putting on new clothes."[24] Baptism also unites us with all followers of Christ. Even though Ali and I didn't speak the same language, as I watched him being baptized, his action communicated the same message my baptism did years ago: "There is one Lord, one faith, one baptism."[25]

As Paul told the church in Corinth, "Some of us are Jews, some are Gentiles, some are slaves, and some are free. But we have all been baptized into one body by one Spirit."[26] In other words, as a follower of Christ, even though you've never met Ali, you're in one family with him. Your baptism is an individual action that unites you with Christ and with a body of believers all over the world.

Teach

Our Great Commission aim isn't just to secure decisions from people to follow Christ, but to make disciples who follow Christ. It's disciples, rather than decisions, that we need to track. That's why Jesus' command is, "Teach these new disciples to obey all the commands I have given you."[27]

Theologian and missiologist Zane Pratt puts it bluntly: "A 'convert' with no commitment to a life of discipleship may very well not be born again at all."[28] That statement might be difficult to swallow, but it's not without precedent. When Jesus communicated the requirements of following him, "many of his disciples turned away and deserted him."[29]

Teaching others to obey the commands of Christ isn't about teaching adherence to religious legalism. It's about teaching others how to live daily under the lordship of Christ and all he taught. As followers of Christ, we are to saturate our minds with Scripture. God's Word transforms how we live our lives and how we see the world.

Disciples are commissioned to learn the truths of Scripture and then teach them to new followers. Here's how David Platt describes "The biblical simplicity of the church":

> Our brothers and sisters around the world . . . just want to lead people to Jesus, gather them together, open up the Word, pray, sing and spur one another on toward Christ, no matter what it costs. . . .
>
> I want to shepherd [my] church in such a way that God could pick up any member from this church, put them anywhere else in the world, and they would know how and have confidence to make disciples and gather with them as a church with only the Word of God and the Spirit of God.[30]

We don't make disciples by migrating them from one small group to the next, as if we are corralling sheep to stay in the flock. We make disciples by raising up sheep who know the Word of God and are confident to leave the flock in order to find other lost sheep and draw them into the fold.

Available but Not Accessible

The gospel is likely very accessible in your community. It might not be acceptable, but it is accessible. There are probably many churches in your area, as well as Christian radio stations, that routinely communicate the gospel message. And if all the Christians in your town were to gather in one place, you'd probably need something like a stadium to fit everyone in. The presence of churches, Christian media, and Christians themselves in North America demonstrates that the gospel is not only available here but also accessible to anyone who wants to hear it. Sadly, this isn't the case everywhere in the world.

In fact, though the salvation message applies to everyone, it remains inaccessible to 3.37 billion people in the world. These billions of people are often referred to as "unreached." David Platt gives a simple definition: "Unreached peoples and places are those among whom Jesus is largely unknown and the church is relatively insufficient to make Jesus known in its broader population without outside help."[31] (Often, there are few if any churches, few if any believers, and sometimes there is no Bible translated into their language.)

Most of these people live in a rectangular area of North Africa, the Middle East, and Asia called the 10/40 Window, located approximately between 10 and 40 degrees north latitude.

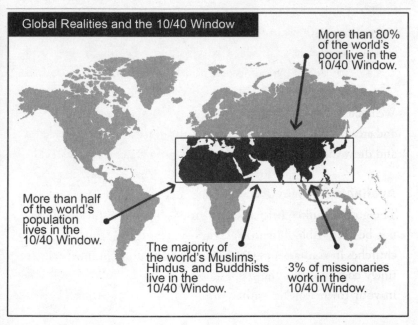

Global Realities and the 10/40 Window

More than 80% of the world's poor live in the 10/40 Window.

More than half of the world's population lives in the 10/40 Window.

The majority of the world's Muslims, Hindus, and Buddhists live in the 10/40 Window.

3% of missionaries work in the 10/40 Window.

There are more people living inside this window than there are in all North America and South America combined. It includes approximately 5.27 billion people, more than half the world's population, and many of the world's major religions reside in this window. Nearly 70 percent of the people groups in this window are considered unreached.[32] I heard one preacher say, "This isn't a window; it's a door of opportunity."

The staggering need to hear the gospel among nearly half the world's population is likely not recognized by most people in your church. But even if it is, it's probably not top of mind. People often filter that information through a Western mindset and say things like, "There are unreached people in my own city."

But the truth is, those people aren't unreached; they're lost. One preacher put it this way: "They aren't unreached because they have you and therefore have access to the gospel."

The 10/40 map should do more than alert us to the global reality of unreached peoples. It should jolt our hearts regarding the eternal certainty of those with no access to the gospel.

But let's get at the root of why so many people in the world remain unreached by looking a little closer to home.

A Lack of Awareness

A 2022 study of US Christians by the Barna Group revealed a significant *lack* of awareness among Christians in three areas: biblical awareness, mission awareness, and global awareness.[33] Listed on the following pages are some of the survey questions and results. Barna segmented Christians into groups based on how often they reported going to church. As you read the study results, keep in mind that if you're in a Western context, these numbers likely reflect the reality in your church as well.

Biblical Awareness

Have you ever heard of the Great Commission?

All US Christians: 63 percent said they had never heard of the Great Commission; 31 percent said they had, but only 12 percent could define it.

Churched Christians (those who attend church once every six months): 48 percent said they had never heard of the Great Commission; only 20 percent said they had and could define it.

Practicing Christians (those who attend church at least once a month): 43 percent said they had never heard of the Great Commission; 26 percent said they had and knew what it meant. Another 27 percent said they had heard of it but could not recall what it was.[34]

Mission Awareness

Is Christ's commission a mandate for all people? Eighty-five percent of pastors believe it is, while only 42 percent of practicing Christians believe that Christ's commission is a mandate for all Christians.[35] That's quite a gap between what leaders of churches believe and what the people in their churches believe!

Global Awareness

When asked about sending missionaries and about awareness of unreached peoples, 60 percent of Christians believe that the church sends the "right amount" of missionaries, but only 13 percent knew the number of unreached people in the world.[36] This begs the question, if they weren't aware of how many unreached people there are and where they are, how could they conclude that the church was sending enough missionaries?

What all these findings clearly reveal is that something needs to change. It needs to change in me, and it needs to change in you. It needs to change in my church, and it needs to change in yours.

It's not that our neighbors don't need Jesus; they do. But the gospel is readily accessible to them through us and through our churches. Lostness is a problem both locally and globally, and the gospel is the solution. But 3.37 billion people with no access to the gospel is a tragedy—an eternal one.

We Must Not Retrench

John and Betty Stam were in their twenties when they moved to China as missionaries in the 1930s. Despite the Communist threat, they were resolute. In a graduation address at Moody Bible Institute in 1932, John said, "Let us remind ourselves that the Great Commission was never qualified by clauses calling for advance only if funds were plentiful and no hardship or self-denial involved. . . . Our way is plain. We must not retrench in any work which we are sure is in His will and for His glory. . . . We must go forward in the face of the impossible, even if we only know the next step."[37]

Eventually, civil war broke out, and the Stams' attempts to leave with their three-month-old daughter, Helen, were unsuccessful. They were arrested and marched twelve miles to a certain death. They passed a local postmaster who asked, "Where are you going?"

"We do not know where they are going, but we are going to heaven," John replied.

The Stams were separated that night. Betty hid Helen in a sleeping bag. The next day John and Betty were stripped naked, paraded through the streets, and later beheaded. Helen was rescued by a Chinese pastor who returned her to her maternal grandparents.

On the morning of their execution, John wrote a letter that was later found bundled among Helen's clothes. Though his words were written one hundred years ago, I pray they seize your heart today: "May God be glorified whether by life or by death."[38]

We must be bold.

God's mission is possible.

5

Radical: God's Unusual Plan with Unlikely People

The frontiers of the kingdom of God were never advanced by men and women of caution.

DOROTHY ANNE MOWLL

MY FRIEND AND I STOOD ON THE TENNIS COURTS with ten Hindu friends who had recently moved to America from India. Don't picture professional tennis players or experts at crossing cultures. We were just a notch above novice at both. We played games, shared our lives, and ate incredible Indian food. Our friendship grew beyond the tennis courts, and we soon began visiting in each other's homes.

When I asked our Indian friends questions about Hinduism, they showed me figurines of their gods. Then they asked me questions about Christianity and why we "drank blood." It may sound like a strange question, but it's also a legitimate one based on Jesus' words, "Unless you eat the flesh of the Son of Man and drink his blood, you cannot have eternal life."[1]

One day, our friends showed up on the courts feeling deeply discouraged. When they explained that another friend had experienced a miscarriage, I sensed God leading me to pray for their friend, aloud, right then.

"May I pray for your friend?" I asked.

In a unanimous chorus, they said, "Yes, please."

I stood on a tennis court with ten Hindu friends praying in Jesus' name.

Do you know what happened afterward?

Nothing.

We played tennis.

A year passed, and several of our friends moved away. One night, I received a message from one of them on Facebook that read, "Do you remember that day you prayed on the tennis court?"

"I do," I replied.

"There was a power present that day that isn't there when I pray. Tell me about that power."

Through the power of his Spirit, God uses unexpected moments and unlikely people in unpredictable ways to accomplish his plan.

The Great Commission in Acts 1:8

In the previous chapter, we looked at the four Great Commission passages recorded in the Gospels. Here, we'll consider the fifth Great Commission passage found in the book of Acts.

Jesus had trained his disciples for three years, but when he handed them the baton of his mission, they still thought the world revolved around them. They asked, "Lord, has the time come for you to free Israel and restore our kingdom?"[2]

I sometimes witnessed this mentality in my children when I gave them chores. Instead of focusing on what I'd asked them to do, they'd ask, "What are you cooking for us for dinner tomorrow?" I wanted to snap my fingers in front of them and say, "Focus!"

Jesus re-centers the disciples' focus on his commission:

> You will receive power when the Holy Spirit comes upon
> you. And you will be my witnesses, telling people about
> me everywhere—in Jerusalem, throughout Judea, in
> Samaria, and to the ends of the earth.
>
> ACTS 1:8

The Sent One became the sender, sending both the Spirit and
the disciples.

There was no discussion concerning their confidence, no nego-
tiation of the terms, no options to consider, and no time to ask
questions. Jesus' words were definitive because he had authority
to deliver on them.

The Great Commission in Acts 1:8 gives us the scope of where
we are to go. We might think of Jesus' reference to Judea, Samaria,
and the ends of the earth in terms of concentric circles, as if Jesus
were saying, "Start local and then work your way out to global."
But if we step into the shoes of the disciples, the places Jesus named
likely sounded more like this:

"Go to Jerusalem and Judea, to people who killed me and
despise you. Also go to Samaria, to the people whom you detest.
And then go to the ends of the earth among people whom you
don't even know exist. Dismissed."

It reminds me of Elisabeth Elliot's words: "If a duty is clear, the
dangers surrounding it are irrelevant."[3]

When Jesus ascended into heaven, he entrusted his followers
with a mission. The mandate was risky. Jerusalem was in an uproar.
But their duty was clear. The dangers were irrelevant.

And when the power of the Holy Spirit came and filled the
believers, everything radically changed.

End of story . . . but the beginning of the church.

Tether Your Confidence to the Spirit

One hundred twenty Jesus followers gathered in a room for one purpose—prayer.

Then something unusual happened. It began with the sound of a roaring wind, ushering in what appeared to be tongues of flame settling on people's heads.[4] Uneducated Galileans, who likely had never traveled beyond their local region, were speaking languages from other places. When people in the city heard the sound, they rushed to the scene. When they arrived, they were all amazed to hear the gospel being spoken in their own languages.[5] After Peter preached the gospel, three thousand people were baptized.[6] What a day!

Don't forget who the disciples were! They were normal nobodies chosen by Christ to be a part of something bigger than them. The Holy Spirit poured out on unlikely people, enabling them to participate in the radical and revolutionary work of God. The Holy Spirit empowered them, giving them confidence to speak and confidence to go. As the renowned nineteenth-century preacher Charles Haddon Spurgeon once observed, "You have said, 'What can I do?' Yes, but when Christ, by His Spirit grips you—what can you *not* do?"[7]

Confidence to Speak

Notice that when the Spirit came, people spoke. Yes, the Holy Spirit is our comforter, counselor, teacher, helper, intercessor, sin-convicter, life-giver, gift-giver, and truth-revealer.[8] But the Spirit also empowers us to speak or prophesy his word! There is evidence of this in both the Old and New Testaments.

OLD TESTAMENT
- Seventy elders: "And when the *Spirit* rested upon them, *they prophesied.*"[9]

- Pagan King Balaam: "Then the *Spirit of God* came upon him, and this is the *message he delivered . . .*"[10]
- King Saul: "Then the *Spirit of God* came powerfully upon Saul, and he, too, began to *prophesy.*"[11]
- Ezekiel: "Then the *Spirit of the Lord* came upon me, and he *told me to say . . .*"[12]

NEW TESTAMENT
- Elizabeth "was filled with the *Holy Spirit . . .* and *exclaimed . . .*"[13]
- Zechariah "was filled with the *Holy Spirit* and gave this *prophecy . . .*"[14]
- Peter, "filled with the *Holy Spirit, said* to them . . ."[15]
- Those in the early church were "all filled with the *Holy Spirit.* Then they *preached* the word of God with boldness."[16]

You are not exempt from the Holy Spirit's empowering work! The apostle Peter said, "What you see was predicted long ago by the prophet Joel: 'In the last days,' God says, 'I will pour out *my Spirit* upon *all people.* Your sons and daughters *will prophesy.*'"[17] *All people* includes you and me!

Allow me to guess what you might be thinking right now: "I'm not extroverted enough, educated enough, or confident enough to tell others about Jesus." If that's what you're thinking, *great*! You're in good company because the disciples weren't any of those things either.

Jesus chose Peter, an overreactor and foot-in-mouth big talker, who betrayed the Lord under pressure. But when the Holy Spirit came upon him, he preached to thousands of people at Pentecost.[18]

Jesus chose John, who along with his brother James, had an anger management problem. These "Sons of Thunder" wanted to call down fire from heaven to burn a Samaritan village. But when the Holy Spirit changed John's heart, he willingly went to many Samaritan villages proclaiming the gospel.[19]

Jesus chose Thomas, whose initial uncertainty about the Resurrection won him the enduring nickname Doubting Thomas. And yet, Christian tradition tells us it was Thomas who earned the long-distance award when, in the power of the Holy Spirit, he confidently took the gospel to India.

Jesus specifically chose a collection of uneducated, mismatched personalities with checkered backgrounds to blaze a gospel trail and ignite the greatest movement in all history.

So why would Jesus not do the same with you?

We need to tether our confidence not to our own abilities but to the power of the Holy Spirit at work within us!

Confidence to Go

When we tether our confidence to the Spirit within us, we have the boldness to *speak* and to move our feet and *go*. After Jesus commissioned his followers to "go and make disciples of all the nations," he added a promising assurance to stoke their confidence: "Be sure of this: I am with you always, even to the end of the age."[20]

So, let us reject passivity and accept the responsibility—with all confidence—that we have been sent to advance the gospel. Our focus is on Jesus, who by his Spirit is always with us.

If we focus on mimicking the church down the street, or find our inspiration only from powerful speakers and podcast personalities, how will we know where the Spirit is leading? Conferences, whiteboard brainstorms, and five-year plans are helpful for gaining insight, sparking creativity, and building strategies. But how the Spirit moves isn't always preplanned, neatly packaged, or easily explained. The Spirit's guidance sometimes defies human logic and leads us to participate in ways we never would have orchestrated on our own. We need look no further than the Bible for examples of how the gospel was taken to Africa, to the Gentiles, and to Macedonia.

HOW THE GOSPEL WENT TO AFRICA

God interrupted Philip's successful city ministry in Samaria to send him to the desert.[21] People were getting saved in the city, but who was in the desert? An Ethiopian who worked as treasurer for the queen of his country. The Holy Spirit said to Philip, "Go over and walk along beside the carriage"—which Philip did. After teaching the Ethiopian man the meaning of Isaiah's prophecy about the Messiah and sharing the gospel with him, Philip baptized him.[22] Talk about evangelizing—and winning to Christ—someone who has influence in a nation! This encounter was bigger than Philip—he could never have arranged such a meeting on his own. It was the Holy Spirit who arranged it and gave him the confidence to go.

HOW THE GOSPEL WENT TO THE GENTILES

As God empowered Peter with a powerful preaching ministry, thousands were saved. Then, God interrupted Peter's momentum by sending him a vision followed by a message from the Holy Spirit: "Three men have come looking for you. Get up, go downstairs, and go with them without hesitation."[23] The men led Peter to Cornelius, an Italian commander in the Roman Army. When Peter preached to Cornelius and his gathered friends and family, a mini-Pentecost happened among the Gentiles. Peter's heart changed toward non-Jews, and he said, "I see very clearly that God shows no favoritism. In every nation he accepts those who fear him and do what is right."[24] Peter didn't initiate this encounter. It was the Holy Spirit who directed it and gave him the confidence to go.

HOW THE GOSPEL WENT TO MACEDONIA

Paul's first missionary journey was a success! He had chosen the destination for his second missionary journey, but the Holy Spirit repeatedly prevented him from traveling there.[25] Then Paul had a vision of a man saying, "Come over to Macedonia."[26] Macedonia was in northern Greece, which meant the gospel was about to go transcontinental for the first time. Paul had made his plans, but the Holy Spirit had a different strategy.

The Holy Spirit is always out ahead of us, arranging the meetings, initiating the encounters, and choosing the destinations to help us get the gospel to the people who need to hear it. And when he sends us, he gives us the confidence we need to speak and go in the power of Jesus' name.

Remember Whose Name Is on the Line

The narrative in chapters 3 and 4 of Acts give us a front row seat to the mystery of the Spirit at work through Peter and John, "ordinary men with no special training in the Scriptures."[27] Their first encounter with the power of the Spirit took place in an ordinary moment as they were on their way to the Temple for afternoon prayer.

Peter and John likely went to the Temple at the same time every day and no doubt had seen the lame man who begged at the same gate every day. But Peter and John were no longer the same men they had once been. They had a new inner power that changed their outer perspective.

This time, when they saw the lame man, they "looked at him intently."[28] The dynamic is reminiscent of the way Jesus had noticed one man in a tree, one paralytic, one crippled woman, and one leper.[29] They saw one man, financially broke and physically and spiritually broken.

Peter got personal. He said to the man, "I don't have any silver or gold for you. But I'll give you what I have." Then Peter put Jesus' name on the line: "In the name of Jesus Christ the Nazarene, get up and walk!"[30] Peter took the man's hand to help him up, and he was instantly healed: "Then, walking, leaping, and praising God, he went into the Temple with them."[31] Talk about picking up someone on your way to church!

Standing amidst an astonished crowd who wondered how the lame man came to walk, Peter made Jesus' name known to them all: "Through faith in the name of Jesus, this man was healed—and you know how crippled he was before. Faith in Jesus' name has healed him before your very eyes. . . . Now repent of your sins and turn to God, so that your sins may be wiped away."[32] In response, "many of the people who heard their message believed it, so the number of men who believed now totaled about 5,000."[33]

Peter and John could have easily overlooked one man in an ordinary moment. Instead, they harnessed that moment in the name of Jesus, and through the explosive power of the Spirit, the landscape of eternity changed for five thousand people.

Here's one more thing to note about this encounter. Peter and John didn't stop at meeting the needs of one man; they also proclaimed the gospel. Today, we're often more comfortable meeting people's needs than we are sharing the gospel. We reason that maybe they'll just "feel" Jesus in us. Theologian Christopher Wright counters this idea, writing, "Mission may not always *begin* with evangelism. But mission that does not ultimately *include* declaring the Word and the name of Christ, the call to repentance, and faith and obedience has not completed its task."[34]

Same Name, Same Task

Just as the disciples did great works in Jesus' name, spoke in Jesus' name, and refused to be silent about Jesus' name, we too have been called to serve in Jesus' name.

We don't have to be concerned about our reputation. We can be confident in Jesus' proven record.

We don't have to fear failure. Jesus said we will receive power through the Spirit.

We don't have to save anyone. We just introduce them to the Savior.

We pray in Jesus' name because he said, "You can ask for anything *in my name,* and I will do it, so that the Son can bring glory to the Father."[35]

We love others in Jesus' name, demonstrating Christ's love and declaring the gospel because "God has given *no other name* under heaven by which we must be saved."[36]

We make disciples of all nations, "baptizing them *in the name* of the Father and the Son and the Holy Spirit."[37]

We go to unreached peoples and places because we know that "*at the name of Jesus* every knee should bow . . . and every tongue declare that Jesus Christ is Lord."[38]

We live our lives in Jesus' name because "whatever [we] do, in word or deed, [we] do everything in the *name of the Lord Jesus.*"[39]

We have access to the same name that empowered the mission of the early church, and we have the same task—to leverage every moment of our lives to share the gospel and make disciples.

There Is Still Power in Jesus' Name

In 2015, Nepal experienced a devastating earthquake that killed more than nine thousand people. A Christian humanitarian relief organization sent resources to build temporary shelters for people who had lost their homes. An area once closed to the gospel was now eager to hear it, and a church started. As one woman said, "Only Christians came to help us."

Two years after the earthquake, I traveled to Nepal with a team. As we gathered with the believers of the new church to sing and worship, a woman came up to me and said, "You need to come. There is a demon-possessed girl."

Now, give me some grace. These are not words I'm accustomed to hearing.

"Maybe you should get the pastor," I responded.

It wasn't long before the whole church stood around the girl, who was now writhing on the ground. Uncertain of the situation, someone from the team said, "Maybe she's having a seizure." Another said, "Maybe she's dehydrated." But the moment the girl looked at us with a contorted face and said, "Get away from me, or I'll eat you," we all began to pray.[40]

For an hour, we prayed aloud in Jesus' name. A larger crowd began to gather, and I found myself questioning, "Jesus, are you going to work? We are putting your name on the line in front of all these people and claiming that you have the power to heal and deliver, and you do! But will you?"

Time passed. Slowly.

When the girl eventually sat up, her demeanor had changed. It reminded me of how the apostle John described the man healed of demon possession as being "in his right mind."[41]

Missionaries all over the world attest to the miraculous ways in which God continues to display his power today. Individuals, families, villages, and cities are being transformed in Jesus' name.

Sometimes It's Okay to Have No Clue

Most newlyweds live with meager means, but Megan and Josh had exactly what they needed—nothing. Fresh out of college, they moved to South Asia, backpacked up into the mountains near a 26,000-foot peak and lived at its base among the local people. They rented a room above an animal stable that was furnished only with a mud stove and a wooden platform bed.

In their words, "We had no clue what we were doing."

The training they received can be summed up in two sentences: If you meet lost people, share the gospel. If you meet believers, disciple them.

If they could have, Megan and Josh would have carried more. But when hiking up an incline while losing oxygen as you gain altitude, carrying extra weight is not an option. As they met people in their new community, they asked if anyone had anything to spare, but few residents had an excess of anything. They didn't realize it at the time, but they were living Jesus' command: "Now go. . . . Don't take any money with you, nor a traveler's bag, nor an extra pair of sandals. . . . Stay in one place, eating and drinking what they provide."[42]

Eventually, one man gave them a teakettle that had a hole in it. What do you do with a broken teakettle? You take it to a blacksmith. What do you do while the blacksmith is patching your teakettle? You wait. And strike up a conversation.

They learned about the blacksmith's grandfather, who had died a year prior. When a Buddhist dies, the family goes to the local lama, a Buddhist spiritual leader, who tells them what rites to perform and how to dispose of the body. The family wanted to take the grandfather's body back to the village where he was born. However, the lama in that village told them something different than their local lama.

Confused, the blacksmith asked, "What is truth? Is it the words of the first or second lama?" Megan and Josh shared that truth was a person, Jesus Christ.

Not only did the blacksmith give his life to follow Jesus, but he was also the first known believer in that people group! He told his family and friends about Jesus, and soon the first church started in an area where many churches exist today.

Like Megan and Josh, when it comes to sharing the gospel, most of us have probably thought at some point, "I have no clue what I'm doing." We are tempted to focus on our inabilities and insecurities and dismiss ourselves from playing any part in God's story. Rarely do we feel capable. But God isn't looking for those who are *able*; he's looking for those who are *available*. When we're available, God can enable us through the Holy Spirit to do great things in his name for his glory. These things may not be predictable; they may pop up in ordinary moments and everyday encounters with others. These things may not be typical, but you can trust that God works in radical ways that can only be explained by him.

6

Global: To the Ends
of the Earth

Foreign missions are not an extra; they are the acid test
of whether or not the church believes the gospel.

LESSLIE NEWBIGIN

IN PREPARATION FOR MENTORING a seminary student for a practicum, I surveyed the required class reading. It was a general ministry class, and the curriculum covered a variety of ministries—small groups, counseling, children's ministry, student ministry, and others. Within each category were questions.

One question in the "world missions" category caught my attention: "How does world missions fit into the programs of a local church?" I understood the intent behind the question, which was to include missions along with other ministries. Though that might sound good, it actually reflects a misalignment. Missions is not something to "fit in" with other ministries; God's global mission is the *core identity* of the church and the foundation for all its other ministries.

To stay on course, the church must align with God's mission. Otherwise it might end up in what missiologist Ed Stetzer calls a "cul-de-sac on the Great Commission highway."[1] The church doesn't drive the Great Commission; the Great Commission drives the church and every ministry of the church.

So, the question is not, "How does world missions fit into the programs of a local church?" but, "How do the ministries of the church align with God's global mission?"

Here's the difference. The original question communicates that "world missions" is one ministry department among many. The better question communicates that God's global mission is why the church exists. Rather than positioning missions as one ministry among many, it demands that every ministry of the church be an extension of God's mission. Pastor Oswald J. Smith puts it bluntly when he says, "Any church that is not seriously involved in helping fulfill the Great Commission has forfeited its biblical right to exist."[2]

A Church Born for Mission

The gospel quickly went global. The early church didn't hold meetings to organize a missions emphasis week, schedule missions trips, or deliberate the theological meaning of the Great Commission. They experienced Christ relationally, were saturated by the Spirit supernaturally, and set off on a course to reach people globally.

By God's orchestration, Jews from every nation were living in Jerusalem when the Holy Spirit came at Pentecost. When they heard their own languages being spoken by the believers, they were amazed and exclaimed, "How can this be? . . . We all hear these people speaking in our own languages about the wonderful things God has done!"[3]

The magnitude of just how far the gospel advanced in one day is worth a visual glance. Look at the locations of all the nations mentioned in Acts 2:9-11. There were people there from regions known today as Iran, Iraq, Turkey, Rome, Italy, Crete, Egypt, Libya, and more.

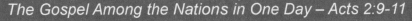

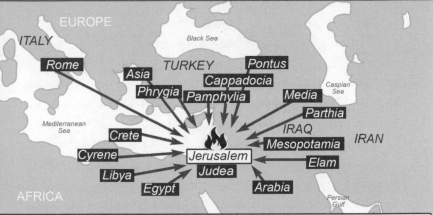

"Here we are—Parthians, Medes, Elamites, people from Mesopotamia, Judea, Cappadocia, Pontus, the province of Asia, Phrygia, Pamphylia, Egypt, and the areas of Libya around Cyrene, visitors from Rome (both Jews and converts to Judaism), Cretans, and Arabs. And we all hear these people speaking in our own languages about the wonderful things God has done!" Acts 2:9-11

God didn't waste time. He used ordinary believers to catapult his plan across ethnic lines and language barriers. And the mission of the first-century church is still the mission for the church today.

Extreme Ownership

It wasn't long before the gospel opportunities of the early church met with opposition. However, though many tried to squelch the momentum of the church, no one could intimidate them. As it says in Acts 6:10 about Stephen, one of the church's first deacons, "They could not stand up against the wisdom the Spirit gave him as he spoke."[4]

Persecution wasn't a surprise. Jesus had told his disciples, "Since they persecuted me, naturally they will persecute you."[5]

And he also said, "But this will be your opportunity to tell them about me."[6]

Persecution was both a tragedy and a triumph.

When a wave of persecution swept over the church, "all the believers except the apostles were scattered."[7]And what did those who were scattered do? "The believers who were scattered preached the Good News about Jesus wherever they went."[8]

Persecution dispersed the believers, but it didn't deter them.

Rulers tried to silence them but emboldened them instead.

Satan tried to quench them but instead kindled the fire within them.

Every believer took extreme ownership of the mission to make Christ's name known. They advanced the cause of Christ regardless of the costs.

The growth of the church was explosive—not because of "professional" disciples or "professional" missionaries but because of ordinary believers scattered throughout the world who proclaimed Christ everywhere they went, lived, shopped, studied, worked, or were imprisoned.

Whose Responsibility Is That Road?

Imagine a dirt road in South Asia lined with many small shops, teahouses, and hostels where town visitors stayed. There, the Christian teachers asked new believers, "Whose responsibility is it to tell people about Jesus along this road?" The teachers didn't give the answer but encouraged the new believers to search the Scriptures. As they flipped through pages of the Bible, they discussed the question among themselves. After much reading and thinking, one person said, "That road is *my* responsibility."

How did this new follower of Jesus discover the answer? What

Scriptures give evidence that all believers have a responsibility to those around them?

The Man That Jesus Wouldn't Allow to Join Him

Jesus crossed cultures when he and the disciples traveled into the region of the Gerasenes, a region inhabited largely by Gentiles. When Jesus stepped out of the boat after crossing the Sea of Galilee, he was approached by a demon-possessed man. Although the local villagers had repeatedly restrained the man with shackles and chains, he smashed them and "wandered among the burial caves and in the hills, howling and cutting himself with sharp stones."[9] When the man saw Jesus, he ran to meet him. "The evil spirits begged [Jesus] again and again not to send them to some distant place."[10] Instead, Jesus cast them into a herd of pigs, "and the entire herd of about 2,000 pigs plunged down the steep hillside into the lake and drowned in the water."[11]

As Jesus was preparing to leave, the man, now "sitting there fully clothed and perfectly sane, . . . begged to go with him. But Jesus said, 'No, go home to your family, and tell them everything the Lord has done for you and how merciful he has been.' So the man . . . began to proclaim the great things Jesus had done for him; and everyone was amazed at what he told them."[12]

Whose responsibility was it to tell the man's family and others in the region about Jesus?

The Woman with a Past

Jesus crossed both cultural and gender divides when he spoke to a Samaritan woman with a sketchy reputation. We already unpacked her story in chapter 3, but notice this: Jesus didn't use an inspirational pep talk to commission her. It was simply her encounter with Jesus that prompted her to go and tell others what had happened to her. The text says she dropped everything and ran to do so:

> The woman left her water jar beside the well and ran back to the village, telling everyone, "Come and see a man who told me everything I ever did! Could he possibly be the Messiah?" So the people came streaming from the village to see him. . . . Many Samaritans from the village believed in Jesus because the woman had said, "He told me everything I ever did!" . . . Then they said to the woman, "Now we believe, not just because of what you told us, but because we have heard him ourselves. Now we know that he is indeed the Savior of the world."[13]

Whose responsibility was it to tell her village about Jesus?

The believers in South Asia came to the same conclusion as the believers in the New Testament. A salvation encounter with Christ leads to extreme ownership of being responsible to tell others around us. Why wouldn't it? The news of salvation in Jesus is too good to keep to ourselves.

What about You?

My second grader came home celebrating. "Mom, I told a boy about Jesus today!" It was a proud mom moment. But then he added, "I asked him what he believed about God, and I told him that if he didn't trust Jesus, he was going to hell."

Well, at least he had great enthusiasm. His approach just needed some work.

Whose responsibility is it to tell people about Jesus at your school? At your gym? On your street? In your office? In your city?

Whose responsibility is it to befriend refugees in your city—the Hindu store owner, the Muslim student, the Sikh Uber driver?

As Bible scholar Christopher Wright points out, "Wherever we go in his name, we are walking on his property. There is not an inch of the planet that does not belong to Christ. Mission[s] then is an authorized activity carried out by tenants on the instructions of the owner of the property."[14]

The property owner of all the earth establishes the boundaries where people live. The apostle Paul writes, "[God] made all the nations, . . . and he marked out their appointed times in history and the boundaries of their lands. God did this so that they would seek him and perhaps reach out for him and find him."[15] Just as it was no coincidence that there were people from many nations living in Jerusalem at Pentecost, it's no coincidence that the ends of the earth may very well be living near you.

The Ends of the Earth Next Door

The nations to which we send missionaries—and are sometimes prevented from sending them—are the same nations whose citizens are moving into our cities. That means we need to know the status of the nations around us. Or as Ralph Winter, founder of the US Center for World Mission, said, "God cannot lead you on the basis of information you do not have."[16]

Look at the map of the nations of foreign-born people who are in the US. Notice that many of them come from an unreached area called the 10/40 Window (see map on page 88). This is not a coincidence. God in his sovereignty uses the movements and plans of humanity for his name and his glory. If God appointed this time in history for people from other nations to live near you, whose responsibility is it to proclaim Jesus to them?

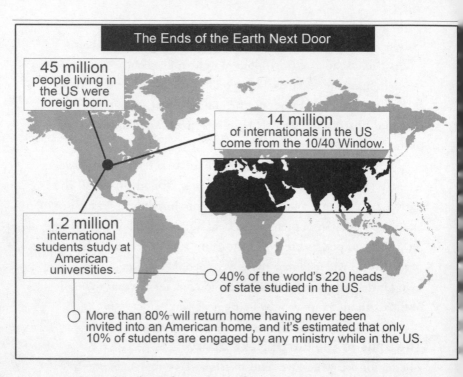

The Ends of the Earth Next Door

45 million people living in the US were foreign born.

14 million of internationals in the US come from the 10/40 Window.

1.2 million international students study at American universities.

40% of the world's 220 heads of state studied in the US.

More than 80% will return home having never been invited into an American home, and it's estimated that only 10% of students are engaged by any ministry while in the US.

Consider these facts about foreign-born people and international students living in the US:

Foreign-Born People

- The US has more immigrants than any other country in the world—about one-fifth of the world's total immigrants.
- 45 million people living in the United States were born in another country.
- More than 14 million of those are from the 10/40 Window, including 12.3 million from Asia and almost 2 million from North Africa and the Middle East.

International Students

- More than 1.2 million international students study in the US each year. It is estimated that 80 percent of them will return to their home countries without ever having been invited into an American home.
- 68 percent of international students are from 10/40 Window countries.
- 40 percent of the world's 220 heads of state once studied in the US.[17]

Why do these statistics matter? Because they demonstrate that you can make a global impact right where you live. A software developer can reach Indian Hindus in California, a stay-at-home mom can reach Afghan Muslims in Virginia, a schoolteacher can reach a Somalian family in Ohio, and a cashier can reach Tibetan Buddhists in New York.

A Muslim at Church

Imagine a Muslim woman showing up at your church on a Sunday morning.

That's how my friend Debbie met Yasemin.

Yasemin grew up Muslim in Central Asia. When she traveled to America as a high school international student, her host family involved her in their activities, including church. Up to that point, she knew about Jesus only from her grandfather, who had an *Injil*. (This is an Arab book containing the four Gospels. It is one of five Muslim holy books.)

When she finished her year in the US, she returned to her home country, got married, and had children. When her children were ready for college, she sent them to study in the United States, where they became American citizens and remained.

Yasemin was visiting her children in the US when she asked them to take her to "a big church with a cross on it" one Sunday morning. That's where Yasemin first met Debbie.

Debbie continued to build a friendship with Yasemin, involving her in holidays and family events. Others in the church invited her into their homes. When Debbie shared the gospel with Yasemin just before Easter, it wasn't the first time or even the second. Debbie had taken advantage of multiple gospel-sharing moments. But it was *this* moment when Yasemin made the decision to give her life to Christ.

God had been pursuing Yasemin for decades—from childhood when she learned about Jesus in her grandfather's *Injil*, to her high school experience as an international student, to her friendship with Debbie. The gospel seed was planted by one and watered by another, and in time it bore fruit.

If God is pursuing the people near us, people like Yasemin, shouldn't we join him?

God's People Love and Care for Foreigners

God's love for us isn't contingent on whether we agree with him or on whether we even believe he exists. Here's the promise of Scripture: "God showed his great love for us by sending Christ to die for us *while we were still sinners.*"[18] God does not call us to love only those who agree with our beliefs, but to love even our enemies.[19] The best way for us to reach those with whom we fundamentally disagree is to begin by loving them well.

No matter where we stand theologically or what our political opinions might be about refugees or immigration, we can't sidestep the huge gospel opportunity in front of us. According to the Bible, a defining characteristic of God's people is how well we love and care for those from other lands.

Love Them

"Do not take advantage of foreigners who live among you in your land. Treat them like native-born Israelites, and love them as you love yourself."[20]

Care for Them

"'Now which of these three would you say was a neighbor to the man who was attacked by bandits?' Jesus asked. The man replied, 'The one who showed him mercy.' Then Jesus said, 'Yes, now go and do the same.'"[21]

Share with Them

"When you are harvesting your crops and forget to bring in a bundle of grain from your field, don't go back to get it. Leave it for the foreigners, orphans, and widows. Then the LORD your God will bless you in all you do."[22]

Comfort Them

"You must not oppress foreigners."[23]

Take Them In

"I was a stranger, and you invited me into your home."[24]

We are not to mimic the way the world treats foreigners. We are to imitate Jesus, who modeled loving foreigners well. How did he interact with them?

- He fed four thousand Gentiles in Decapolis (Mark 8:1-9).
- He healed the Roman centurion's servant (Luke 7:1-10).
- He had compassion for a demon-possessed Gentile man (Mark 5:1-20).

- He went out of his way to talk with a Samaritan woman (John 4:1-42).
- He spoke truth but didn't debate Pilate, the Roman governor (John 18–19).
- He used a story of a foreigner's generous giving to make a point to religious people concerning who is a good neighbor (Luke 10:25-37).

Love like Jesus loved. When we love well, we prove that we are Christ followers. Jesus said, "Your love for one another will prove to the world that you are my disciples."[25]

Steps to Welcoming

As Heather's small group talked about the nations represented in their city, she mentioned a Muslim family from the Middle East living in her neighborhood. Every day she saw the mother at the school bus stop when they each picked up their children. Heather said, "I never talk to her because I don't know what to say."

A lot of us can relate to Heather. We don't know where to start, so we never begin. But the steps to welcoming and building friendships with internationals aren't that complicated. Here are eight principles to help you get started:

Initiate. Be aware of who is around. Sit by them, go to their checkout counter, play at the same park, or buy goods at their store. Be intentional. Then, start with hello. It's easy! We fear not knowing what to say when one of the best things we can do is demonstrate love by being friendly. You're not seeking a bait-and-switch relationship—trying to befriend them just so you can present the gospel. You're simply being intentional about building an authentic friendship. In the words of the apostle Paul, "Don't just pretend to love others. Really love them."[26]

Invest. Genuinely loving people requires getting to know them personally. Be interested in them because, like you, they are God's creation. Questions are a great way to get to know someone. For example, what is their home country? What brought them to America? How do they spell their name? How many are in their family? Listen and take an interest. Also, this is not an interrogation, so share about yourself as well.

Invite. Americans tend to value their schedules, whereas many other cultures value time together. Demonstrate hospitality by making room in your busy life to extend hospitality. Invite people over for tea, a meal, or to play games. Include internationals in your holiday and family celebrations.

Integrate. Be a learner. Notice the practices of their culture. For example, do they take off their shoes when entering a home, eat with their hands or utensils, or greet one another differently than you do? Learn to be comfortable in their environment and willing to honor their customs. And keeping a sense of humor is almost always an asset when it comes to loving well. Learn to laugh at yourself as you discover the differences between your culture and theirs.

Interact. Take your friendship to a new level by introducing your international friends to your American friends. Doing so communicates that they are part of your circle. It also creates an opportunity for your friends to interact with another culture and opens a door for your international friends to invite you into their friendship circles.

Intervene. Not everyone will tell you when they have a need. Many internationals feel lonely as they adapt to a new culture. Be observant. Give an appropriate gift to communicate that you care. Make them a meal. If your friend is Muslim, make sure the food is halal. If they are Hindu, check to see if they are vegetarians. Or you might give them something from your home that has meaning. Even a simple plant communicates thoughtfulness.

Intercede. Think big picture by recognizing that God is always at work. Pray and ask the Holy Spirit to create an awareness in your heart of divine moments to show love and share Jesus.

Introduce. Religion plays an important role in most people's lives. Ask them to tell you about their spiritual journey. Ask if you can share yours. Most will already assume that you're a Christian because you're from the West.

These steps are not in a specific order. But every one represents a way to build bridges of trust that can bear the weight of truth.

Exercise Gospel Intelligence

Let's just call them First Church Anytown.

The Muslim refugee population was increasing in their city, and the church decided to host a back-to-school backpack drive to provide necessary supplies for refugee children. In addition to giving away the backpacks, they also planned to have a brief service to share the gospel. On the day of the event, hundreds of backpacks were stuffed with school items and put neatly on display. A crowd of refugees filled the church parking lot, parents accepted the donated backpacks, and then everyone quickly left.

Instead of seeing the event as a success—that they had served these refugee families well by providing for them—the church leader in charge said, "We'll never do that again. No one stayed for the message, and not one has ever attended our church."

The church leader concluded that the event was a failure. But if the church had exercised gospel intelligence in a diverse cultural situation, they might have found it to be the beginning of a new relationship. Serving people is often a longtime process, not a onetime event.

Serve people, but realize that people aren't projects.

You know the Savior, but you're not a Jesus salesman.

Just as we love Scripture and desire to exegete, or interpret, it carefully, we need to "exegete" the cultures of those we hope to reach. Gospel intelligence is what enables us to identify an opportunity in the midst of religious and cultural diversity to share the gospel effectively. We exercise gospel intelligence when we first consider what the barriers to the gospel might be, and also what bridges we might need to build to effectively communicate the gospel.[27] Many missionaries have practiced this kind of gospel intelligence for years.

Paul exercised gospel intelligence when he entered Athens. His heart was broken when he saw that the city was full of idols. He shared Christ with Jews, God-fearing Greeks, and groups of philosophers. He met in their synagogues and in the streets. He was on their turf and "exegeted" what he'd witnessed in their culture. He started with something that was familiar and built a bridge to the gospel. "I notice that you are very religious in every way, for as I was walking along I saw your many shrines. And one of your altars had this inscription on it: 'To an Unknown God.' This God, whom you worship without knowing, is the one I'm telling you about."[28]

His approach wasn't to have a onetime encounter or even one conversation. He "spoke daily in the public square to all who happened to be there."[29] The way that he exercised gospel intelligence led to decisions to follow Christ and left an open door for those who still wanted to hear more. "When they heard Paul speak about the resurrection of the dead, some laughed in contempt, but others said, 'We want to hear more about this later.'"[30]

God is working to make himself known to people. And even though people continually move from one country to another, God is not chasing them; he is choreographing their movement. He is doing this, as Paul told the people in Athens, so that nations will "seek after God and perhaps feel their way toward him and find him."[31] God desires the gospel to reach the ends of the earth. And the ends of the earth are near you!

7

Unstoppable: A Church beyond Borders and Barriers

We must be global Christians with a global vision
because our God is a global God.

JOHN R. W. STOTT

IT WAS A MASSIVE INTERNATIONAL UNDERTAKING. After nine days without contact, twelve boys aged eleven to sixteen and their twenty-five-year-old coach were found alive in the flooded Tham Luang cave in northern Thailand. Trapped by rising waters, the thirteen had found temporary safety on a small patch of high ground deep within the cave. With merciless rains continuing, time was running out.

In the beginning, no one knew what to do. Rescuers went to work figuring out how to extract thirteen people, most of whom couldn't swim. To locate the group, two British divers had traversed four kilometers of winding, flooded caves that would cause even the most experienced diver to struggle.

An army of people was mobilized, and each person's contribution was vital to the mission's success. Engineers worked to pump water out of the cave. More professional divers arrived from various countries. Airlines offered free flights to rescuers. Businesses contributed food, transportation, and equipment. Elon Musk offered technology. Local villagers contributed their knowledge and pitched in what they could. People worldwide who had never heard of Tham Luang cave gave money, and many others prayed for people they had never met. Everyone felt a sense of urgency in the mission.

The day a former Thai Navy SEAL died while attempting to navigate the cave system amplified the danger everyone faced. The risk was real, but lives were at stake.

Everyone around the world continually checked for updates. Finally, seventeen days after the boys and their coach went missing, they were saved.

Instead of grieving a tragedy, the world celebrated a rescue that became a story of hope.[1]

The Rescue Operation in Front of Us

The church today has a massive international undertaking. It has a rescue mission and a story of hope. It demands that we operate with the same sense of urgency and collaboration demonstrated by the Tham Luang cave rescuers to get the gospel to unreached people.

During the pandemic, I heard a Christian leader say, "Because of COVID-19, missions is on pause." Another said, "Maybe now we'll focus more on local missions rather than global missions."

God's mission is not on pause! Never has been. Never will be. And therefore, the mission of the church is not on pause. There is no viral infection, no political oppression, no forced migration, no military opposition, no geographical limitation, and no religious persecution that can disrupt God's global mission.

If COVID did anything, it caused us to reevaluate whether our ministry was really expanding the Kingdom. Were we doing evangelism or just gospel marketing? Were we making disciples or just planning events? Were we taking the gospel to the nations, or did we just love traveling? What else can be done? How else can we encourage indigenous leaders and churches? How can we creatively use technology to reach the ends of the earth?

Missions might look different now. And probably should. But the mission never ceases.

Shouldn't our posture be like that of the rescue workers at Tham Luang? If one rescue method ceases to work, let us tirelessly and innovatively search for another.

How is it that thirteen lives trapped in a cave stirs us, keeps us on the edge of our chairs, causes us to pull out our wallets, prompts us to use social media to show solidarity, and yet many of us are barely moved by the reality that 42.5 percent of the world has little to no access to the gospel and no eternal hope unless someone comes with a saving message?[2]

In the previous chapter, we looked at reaching people from the ends of the earth who live near us. Yet we must also be concerned with getting the gospel to those who live far from us. This worldwide rescue mission must become our urgent priority.

A Model Church

It seems fitting that the first international church, planted by strategic cross-cultural evangelism, would be the first church to send out missionaries.[3] It was the church at Antioch, not the church at Jerusalem, that inaugurated global missions.

How did the church at Antioch come to be? When the believers scattered due to persecution, many preached the gospel, but only to the Jews. Then, a new development occurred because of men that pastor Timothy Keller calls "mavericks," and theologian John Stott refers to as "daring spirits."[4]

> Some of the believers who went to Antioch from Cyprus and Cyrene [North Africa] began preaching to the Gentiles about the Lord Jesus. The power of the Lord was with them, and a large number of these Gentiles believed and turned to the Lord.[5]

These evangelists traveled from Africa to Antioch to preach the gospel to the Greeks. Although we don't know their names, it was these "daring spirits" who initiated international missions before the apostle Paul was sent out.

Antioch wasn't a *multi*cultural church. It was an *inter*cultural church. To be multicultural is to have diverse cultures that politely function side by side. To be intercultural is to have diversity characterized by intentional and mutual learning from one another. In its diversity, the church in Antioch lived in unity and partnered together in God's mission.

We are partners in the gospel, co-laborers with Christ.[6]

Today, we can co-labor together in unity for the cause of Christ when we send obediently, go strategically, pray audaciously, give generously, and partner wisely.

Send Obediently

I'm sure we would all nod our heads in agreement on hearing Paul's words, "Everyone who calls on the name of the LORD will be saved."[7]

Yes! That's right! Preach it, brother!

But what about when Paul adds some follow-up questions? Would we still be nodding our heads when Paul asks, "How can they call on him to save them unless they believe in him? And how can they believe in him if they have never heard about him? And how can they hear about him unless someone tells them? And how will anyone go and tell them without *being sent*?"[8]

The church in Antioch set the pace for sending internationally. They were consumed with a passion to advance the gospel because they were first focused on exalting Jesus Christ.

"Churches that impact the world exalt Jesus passionately and seek him in prayer dependently and expectantly."[9] In Acts 13:2-3, we see the church at Antioch worshiping and fasting before sending Barnabas and Paul on their first missionary journey together.

Sending is much more than a church commissioning service. The church was disciplined in worship, prayer, and fasting. The scope of these activities suggests that the commissioning of Barnabas and Paul wasn't a quickly scheduled meeting or a time of prayer tacked on at the end of a worship gathering; rather, it was part of the routine practice of a passionate, diverse community united in mission. As the people worshiped and fasted, the Spirit spoke about who to send. After the Spirit spoke, there was "more fasting and prayer."[10]

Today, we are prone to think of sending as something that organizations and agencies do. Agencies can play an important role in sending, but the ultimate responsibility belongs to the church. Notice that worship, prayer, and fasting happened before *and* after the Spirit spoke. Commissioning people to be sent involves much more than a quick segment in a worship service. Much prayer was the foundation to sending. And prayer is the ongoing commitment by the whole church for those who are commissioned and sent out.

Sending identifies and equips people. It was in the context of worship and fasting that the Holy Spirit spoke and identified who should be sent. Jesus modeled this same approach. He spent all night praying before identifying the twelve disciples he would designate as apostles and send out to proclaim the Good News.[11] He told them in the beginning that they would learn to fish for people. He equipped them and then sent them. Jesus was clear: "As the Father has sent me, so I am sending you."[12]

It doesn't matter whether your church is filled with college students, families, or retirees. It doesn't matter whether your church is white collar or blue collar. Who does God desire to be set apart and sent? Who, like Paul and Barnabas, is a faithful disciple, active in ministry? Who is your church equipping to go?

Sending assumes taking responsibility to provide relentless support. Before sailing to India, missionary William Carey and several others were discussing the importance of the mission, but they also saw it as akin to "penetrating into a deep mine, which had never before been explored, [with] no one to guide [them]."[13] Finally, Carey said to his friends, "Well, I will go down, if you will hold the rope."[14]

Whose role was more important—the one holding the rope or the one going down into the pit? Consider it this way: Whose role is more important in war? The ones doing the fighting on the front lines? Or the ones funding the soldiers? Or the ones supplying ammunition? Or the ones taking care of the soldiers' physical and mental health?

Advancing the gospel requires both sending and going. Every missionary needs a rope holder. And every church needs to hold the rope for someone sent.

Go Strategically

Many of us will not move overseas to take the gospel to unreached peoples. But before you insert yourself into the "many of us" category, let me ask you, "Are you called to stay?" If your answer is *yes*, what role do you play? It's been my experience that 99.9 percent of Christians "feel called to stay," even as 42.5 percent of the world has no access to the gospel. It makes me wonder whether God is no longer calling or if we're not listening.

Nevertheless, every one of us is under joyous obligation to participate in the salvation of souls here and there, and to live our lives for nothing less than the glory of God in all the earth.

The call for Paul and Barnabas was to go, but it wasn't clear where they were supposed to go. God doesn't always give us full instructions, just a simple invitation. As we take the first step of obedience, God reveals the next. As Paul and Barnabas obeyed, they strategically went to places the gospel had not been and leveraged their vocation and skills along the way.

Go Where God's Name Isn't Yet Known

Today, nearly half the world lacks access to the gospel. Paul's ambition was "to preach the Good News where the name of Christ has never been heard, rather than where a church has already been started by someone else."[15] Whether we are the ones who send or go, our ambition for how and where we live our lives should be shaped by Christ's mission.

There are approximately 400,000 Christians who are considered missionaries—those who have moved somewhere else for the spread of the gospel. But only about 3 percent (11,000–12,000) of those 400,000 have been sent to unreached people groups.[16] Though we should in no way discount the good work underway in other parts of the world, let us consider where the need for missionaries is the greatest.

The world population continues to increase. As it does, the unreached population outpaces the sending of workers to those regions. We must prioritize going where God's name isn't yet known.

Go, but Don't Quit Your Day Job

You don't have to quit your job to become a "professional missionary." Instead, move your career overseas. Possibilities still exist! Think creatively and globally. Can you do your job in another location? Many countries do not have access to the gospel and refuse to allow missionaries to enter, but they will welcome entrepreneurs, nurses, teachers, baristas, restaurant owners, movie producers, and many other professionals. Your job may provide an opportunity to enter countries where missionaries can't. As far back as 1971, pioneer missionary William Danker addressed the issue of *vocation* as it pertains to missionary service:

> Early in the history of Protestant missions we find important missionary efforts taking a . . . sympathetic view of economic activities. In some cases economic activities became the mainstay of missionary support; in others they provided significant assistance. . . .
>
> The most important contribution of the Moravians was their emphasis that every Christian is a missionary and should witness through his daily vocation. If the example of the Moravians had been studied more carefully by other Christians, it is possible that the businessman might have retained his honored place within the expanding Christian world mission, beside the preacher, teacher, and physician.[17]

The gifts and skills that you have are not an accident. They were given to you by God. As Paul says in Ephesians 2:10, "We are God's masterpiece. He has created us anew in Christ Jesus, so we can do the good things he planned for us long ago." Certainly you can use your job where you are to make a Kingdom impact. But what if your job is a springboard to launch you into unreached places to work among people who have no access to the gospel? A change in location is optional, but God's mission is not.

Pray Audaciously

When I was young, I hated sitting at the kiddie table at Thanksgiving. I wanted to sit at the adult table with important people discussing significant things.

Today, I think many of us consider prayer to be the "kiddie" version of participating in missions. Ask any missionary what you can do to support their work, and they will inevitably reply, "Pray." And they mean it. These people live on the front lines of spiritual war, and they need strong support from the home base calling for firepower from heaven. Paul told the church in Corinth, "You are helping us by praying for us."[18] Pastor John Piper put it this way, "God has given us prayer as a wartime walkie-talkie so that we can call headquarters for everything we need as the kingdom of Christ advances in the world. Prayer gives *us* the significance of frontline forces and gives *God* the glory of a limitless Provider. The one who gives the power gets the glory."[19]

Often, we don't know what to pray other than, "God bless all the missionaries." But we can always pray intentionally based on Scripture and on world events.

Pray Intentionally Based on Scripture

Pastor Andrew Murray, who said that "missions are the chief end of the church," [20] also said that "the man who mobilizes the Christian church to pray will make the greatest contribution to world evangelization in history." [21] But how do we know what to pray for? Scripture directs us how to pray. When we don't know specifically what to pray for, we can pray the words of Scripture on behalf of missionaries. Here are several examples:

God, open doors. "Pray for us, too, that God will give us many opportunities to speak about his mysterious plan concerning Christ. . . . Pray that I will proclaim this message as clearly as I should." [22]

God, save more. "The longing of my heart and my prayer to God is for the people of Israel to be saved." [23]

God, send more. "So pray to the Lord who is in charge of the harvest; ask him to send more workers into his fields." [24]

God, send far. "My ambition has always been to preach the Good News where the name of Christ has never been heard." [25]

God, be honored. "Pray that the Lord's message will spread rapidly and be honored wherever it goes, just as when it came to you." [26]

God, help them endure. "We are pressed on every side by troubles, but we are not crushed. We are perplexed, but not driven to despair. We are hunted down, but never abandoned by God. We get knocked down, but we are not destroyed. . . . So we live in the face of death, but this has resulted in eternal life for you. . . . And as God's grace reaches more and more people, there will be great thanksgiving, and God will receive more and more glory. That is why we never give up."[27]

God, give them supernatural power. "And the Lord proved their message was true by giving them power to do miraculous signs and wonders."[28]

Pray Intentionally Based on World Affairs

"The world is falling apart." I recently heard this common phrase from a friend who lamented the shortage of restaurant workers and an empty shelf of cereal items at the local grocery store. I promise that the world isn't falling apart because Cheerios aren't on the shelf. We often view the world through a myopic lens.

If we are to pray intelligently for the world, we must recognize that there's more than one reality. There's the reality that you and I live in, and there are realities that others live in. As I type, most of the news headlines on my television are filled with stories happening within the borders of my own country. Political parties argue, news of inflation continues, and a boy who rescued a dog is celebrated. In world news, wars are raging, Bible translation is needed in thousands of languages, Iranians are reaching Afghans for Christ, food shortages in Sri Lanka are increasing, people are being trafficked to Cambodia, and pastors were arrested in India. In the introduction of this book, we considered William Carey's advice of having "an open Bible and an open map." Perhaps we should possess three tools to help guide us: a Bible, a map, and a source for world news.

Staying informed doesn't take a lot of time. Start by downloading a world missions prayer app, such as Operation World, that suggests one people group a day to pray for. Open Doors also has an app to help you be vigilant in praying for persecuted believers. If you're not into apps, there's also an Operation World book that will guide you in how to pray. Or you can subscribe to a daily email through the Joshua Project that does the same. Choose tools that will build your awareness as you seek to be vigilant in global prayer.

Give Generously

Generous giving reorients our hearts from focusing on the little we have to considering the most we can possibly give. Open your hands and your heart will follow. Paul wrote that the church in Corinth gave out of their nothingness and experienced fullness: "Their abundance of joy and their extreme poverty have overflowed in a wealth of generosity on their part. For they gave according to their means, as I can testify, and beyond their means."[29]

Giving is more than supporting; it's partnering to further the Kingdom. That's why Paul continually encouraged churches to give.

It's also important to consider where you give. Churches spend approximately 99 percent of their missions resources in places that have already been reached with the gospel. Or, to flip it around, churches spend only 1 percent of their missions resources among the over 3 billion people who haven't yet heard the gospel.[30] Or, to make it more personal, for every $100,000 that Christians make, they give $1.70 to the unreached.[31]

Partner Wisely

Find ways to contribute to long-term, strategic work among unreached people and remain committed in your support. At the beginning of my church's global involvement, our approach was scattered with many projects in many places. When we shifted to focus on two partnerships, our giving became more generous, our praying grew more fervent, and our going and sending increased.

Involve the whole church. A focused effort will inspire the participation of the entire congregation. Think creatively and include children, students, and families. In sermons and small groups, communicate what God is doing in the church's missions partnerships. You'll find that people will begin asking about the people group your church is partnering to reach. Lead your church to send long-term workers and short-term teams.

Train for short-term involvement. Many churches send short-term missions teams[32] somewhat haphazardly, as if they were throwing darts at a target while blindfolded. Instead, we need to send teams in partnership with ongoing work in strategic places. That's how we equip teams to think like missionaries rather than tourists.

Tourists think: I can't wait to see the world.
Missionaries think: I can't wait to see what God is doing in the world.

Tourists think: What can I take on my trip to make me more comfortable?
Missionaries think: What can I do to make the people around me more comfortable?

Tourists think: I'd like to fix all the problems I see.
Missionaries think: I'd like to know what the people of the culture think the problems are.

Tourists think: I'm fascinated by how different your culture is from mine.

Missionaries think: I want to live among you and learn your way of life.

Tourists think: I am on a mission to export my faith and convert people.

Missionaries think: I'm joining with God, who is already at work among the people.

Let those with whom we partner say as Paul did to the church at Philippi, "You have been my partners in spreading the Good News about Christ."[33]

You're Not Crazy

People who radically rearrange their lives to align with the cause of Christ have often been considered crazy—crazy for leaving their families, giving too much money, spending their retirement overseas, fasting and praying for hours into the night, or going to dangerous places. My grandmother thought my husband and I were crazy for taking her great-grandchildren overseas.

People thought the apostle Paul was crazy too. He wrote, "Because we understand our fearful responsibility to the Lord, we work hard to persuade others. God knows we are sincere. . . . If it seems we are crazy, it is to bring glory to God. And if we are in our right minds, it is for your benefit. Either way, Christ's love controls us."[34]

When nineteenth-century Scottish missionary John Paton told his church that he sensed God sending him to live among a tribe in the South Pacific, many responded as if he were insane. Among those who attempted to deter him was an older man whose continual argument was, "The cannibals! You will be eaten by cannibals!"

Paton replied, "Mr. Dickson, you are advanced in years now, and your own prospect is soon to be laid in the grave, there to be eaten by worms; I confess to you that if I can but live and die serving and honoring the Lord Jesus, it will make no difference to me whether I am eaten by cannibals or by worms; and in the Great Day my resurrection body will arise as fair as yours in the likeness of our risen Redeemer."

Still, others posed an argument we still hear today: "There are heathen at home. Let us seek and save, first of all, the lost ones perishing at our doors." But Paton admitted, "This I felt most true, and an appalling fact; but I unfailingly observed that those who made this retort neglected these home Heathen themselves; and so the objection, as from them, lost all its power."[35]

People may observe any action we take to further the cause of Christ and deem it abnormal. We are in good company when we are mocked or insulted for our radical obedience to God's mission. It's all worth it because souls are in jeopardy unless we become the beautiful feet that bring the Good News to them.

Our vision must always align with a missionary God whose global aim for his glory is unstoppable. The church cannot fail. Our aim is global because God's aim is global.

8

Historical: The State
of the World

*As I travel, I have observed a pattern, a strange historical
phenomenon of God "moving" geographically from the
Middle East to Europe, to North America, to the developing
world. My theory is this: God goes where He's wanted.*

PHILIP YANCEY

IMAGINE A CHURCH that sends 2,158 of its members overseas.
Immediately, you might be thinking, "That must be a large church.
They must have a lot of money!" Spoiler alert: It's not—and they
don't. Let's carry on.

Imagine that the people sent overseas support themselves financially by pursuing work in their adopted land. Desiring to make
a gospel, economic, and social impact in their new communities,
they work alongside the people of that country as equals. They
meet dangers with courage and dare to learn languages without
special training. Even though 75 of the first 160 people sent to
one country died, the church keeps sending more. The church is
so committed to Great Commission endeavors that the people vow
to pray 24/7—and not just for a week or a month, but for more
than one hundred years!

Meet the Moravian Brethren, a group of refugees who fled religious persecution in Central Europe in 1722 and found shelter in Saxony on the estate of a wealthy Lutheran nobleman, Count Nikolaus von Zinzendorf. Zinzendorf and the Moravians made one of the most significant contributions in the history of missions.

Nikolaus Zinzendorf was only ten years old when he dedicated his life to taking the gospel to the nations. Being of noble birth, however, he knew that the only acceptable vocation was to study law and eventually work in state service. Side note: Don't underestimate the power of leading children to understand God's mission. Certainly, help them consider what they want to be when they grow up. But also lead them to consider where they might live to do that job in the world.

As Zinzendorf wrestled with his vocation, he came across a painting of Christ in an art gallery. His heart was burdened when he read the inscription, "All this I did for you. What are you doing for me?"

Five years after the first refugees arrived, Zinzendorf met two men from Greenland and another man, an enslaved African from the West Indies, who begged for missionaries to come to their lands. This urgency gripped Zinzendorf's soul and the Moravian church that was experiencing a spiritual renewal. Two young men (a potter and a carpenter) were the first missionaries sent out by the Moravian church to the West Indies, and they worked willingly among the enslaved people. Eventually, more workers moved overseas, including entire families. This continued for decades.

Fifty years after the Moravian church sent the first two men to the West Indies, thirteen thousand converts had been baptized, and churches had been planted on six different islands.[1]

Now, before it sounds like I'm elevating Zinzendorf to saint-hood, as many missionary stories can appear to do, allow me to acknowledge that he also made some poor leadership decisions that nearly caused the movement to collapse. Nevertheless, the Moravian movement, stirred by Zinzendorf's commitment to making Christ's name known, "launched a worldwide missionary movement that set the stage for William Carey and the 'Great Century' of missions that would follow."[2]

The Moravian church itself never grew past a few hundred, in part because it kept sending all its people to other places. But it was a church consumed with a passion for God's mission. Their modus operandi was simple. All Christ followers are missionaries and have the responsibility to participate in spreading the gospel to places it has not yet gone.

Today, Western churches send out an abundance of people to serve short-term missions assignments that have great value. But only one out of every 209,086 Christians goes as a missionary to live among the unreached.[3] That's not even close to the Moravians, who sent one out of every eleven church members as a missionary.

Where are those Christians who are ready to live and die for the call of Christ? Are we raising a soft generation with no zeal for God's Kingdom? We need people with spiritual grit who will pick up the torch of the cause of Christ and choose to live in tough places among unreached people, both poor and affluent, around the globe. We need men and women who will move to global cities and live among the people who have no one else to speak gospel truth into their lives.

God Is at Work in Missions History

As Christians, we are part of the most significant movement of all time, and yet we rarely think of it that way. Theologian Lesslie Newbigin writes,

World Christianity is the result of the great missionary expansion of the last two centuries. That expansion, whatever one's attitude to Christianity may be, is one of the most remarkable facts of human history. One of the oddities of current affairs . . . is the way in which the event is so constantly ignored or undervalued.[4]

Follow the river of God's movement through the landscape of history, and you'll find that he truly is covering the whole earth with his glory. The waters of his glory maneuver around mountains of governments and through valleys of persecution. The waters of his glory topple world leaders and engulf man-made world systems, twisting them into tools he uses for his global purpose.

Where is Artemis, the great goddess the Ephesians worshiped?[5] Gone and largely forgotten.

Where is Nero, who beheaded Paul and persecuted believers? Gone, a mere footnote in Christian history.

Where is Decius, who declared that all Christians must pay homage to Roman gods or die? Gone, along with the gods he worshiped.

Where are those who burned William Tyndale at the stake, attempting to stop the translation and publication of the Bible in English? Gone, but the Bible lives on.

Where is the church today? Alive throughout the world. "The gates of hell shall not prevail against it."[6]

God created history. He arranged the past, and he orchestrates the future. John Stott writes, "History is not a random flow of events. For God is working out in time a plan which he conceived in a past eternity and will consummate in a future eternity."[7] Missions history invites us to lean in and worship as it traces the hand of God, weaving a gospel tapestry that blankets all nations.

There's Never Been a Movement like It

Picture a globe in your mind and imagine turning it as we proceed.

Begin with Israel at the epicenter. Imagine a stream of Christianity spreading out from Israel to Europe in the West and a few other streams of faith extending to North Africa, Central Asia, and the Middle East. Keep in mind that this spreading of faith was something new in human history. Until the first century of the modern era, no people other than Israel believed in the one true God, much less the idea of one true religion.[8]

Three hundred years after Christ, Christianity had spread to every major province of the Roman Empire.[9] Historian Ramsay MacMullen notes that if the church had fizzled out after the first century, its presence would not have been noticed. But "three centuries later, it had successfully displaced or suppressed the other religions of the empire's population."[10]

Now turn your globe toward Europe. Five hundred years after Christ, the epicenter of Christianity had moved to Europe, where the Christian faith became both popular and nominal. While Christianity continued to move into middle Europe, it also began losing ground to Islam across Africa, the Middle East, and on into Spain.

Now pause. Missions historian Kenneth Scott Latourette, calls the next millennium (500–1500) a "thousand years of uncertainty."[11] During the Dark Ages, the church in Europe grew in political wealth and influence but lost its zeal for missions. Politics and Christianity merged, twisting the truths of the gospel.

Just checking to see if you're still with me. Are you asleep? Well, so were the Christians for one thousand years. So, wake up, and let's move on.

Turn the globe again.

The epicenter moved from Europe to North America.
Beginning in the 1500s with the Protestant Reformation in
Europe, the gospel awakened and eventually spread to North
America. The commitment to missions was reignited in Europe
by the Moravians beginning in the 1700s, and spiritual revival
was stirred by two Great Awakenings—the first in Britain and the
American colonies (1730–1755), and the second in the United
States (1795–1835). By the year 1900, missionaries were on every
continent.[12] The past two centuries have witnessed the greatest
missionary movement in history.

Some of the missionary giants from this era include names
you may be familiar with—William Carey, William and Catherine
Booth, Ann and Adoniram Judson, Hudson Taylor, Lottie Moon.
These men and women were the backbone of missions societies
and organizations such as the Salvation Army, the London Bible
Society, Wycliffe Bible Translators, and many others.

Today, there are over 400,000 missionaries worldwide. That's
worth celebrating, but it's also worth asking why only 3 percent of
them are working in the world's most unreached places.

Today, the epicenter has shifted again. In 1910, what is
called the Global North contained 80 percent of the world's
Christians. But today, 67 percent of the world's Christians reside
in the Global South.[13] The Global South is also often referred to
as the Majority World. "With the median age of the global human
population hovering near 31," writes global missions expert Ryan
Shaw, "most people alive today were *born into* a world where the
Christianity as 'the white man's religion' is a relic of the past."[14]
Thank goodness!

As you turn your globe, I hope you can see how the promise
of God filling the earth with his glory is being realized. Truly, as
the psalmist says, "The whole earth will acknowledge the LORD

and return to him. All the families of the nations will bow down before him."[15]

Globalization as Opportunity

The Amazon River pushes out enough water flow daily to provide New York City with electricity for nine years. That's powerful!

In Manaus, Brazil, two dramatically different rivers converge at a site called in Portuguese, *Encontro das Águas*, or "the Meeting of the Waters." It's where the blackest river in the world, Rio Negro, meets up with the light brown waters of Rio Solimões. I flew over the site, and it looked like tar and caramel flowing together into one river, the Amazon.

Globalization is a powerful convergence of cultures, economies, and ideologies flowing together into one channel. This world system creates a wide-open door for the gospel. Indeed, there are pros and cons to globalization, just as the *Pax Romana* of the Roman Empire had pros and cons. The *Pax Romana*, which is Latin for "Roman Peace," was a roughly two-hundred-year period of relative peace and stability. During that time, the Romans built infrastructure, such as aqueducts and roads. The roads proved to be a great export system, which enabled the gospel to flow quickly to many locations. God can use globalization in our day to do the same. God, in his sovereignty, uses human plans for his glory.

With the birth of globalization, we have more economic advantage, transportation access, and innovative technology to leverage for gospel advancement than ever before. We can meet in real time with church leaders thousands of miles away through online streaming or take a plane and land nearly anywhere in the world within twenty-four hours. We can access headlines from around the world that arrive almost as quickly as the events occur.

I recently spoke with an Islamic Uber driver who told me that everything he learned about Christianity he learned from YouTube. I sat with an Afghan refugee friend who was learning how to speak English on TikTok. Economists, anthropologists, sociologists, and even missiologists, are all in wonder about the impact globalization will have on the future.

Thinking global, however, should not be a new phenomenon for the church! Care and concern for a global community was established by God at the beginning when he said, "Be fruitful and multiply and fill the earth and subdue it."[16]

It was confirmed by King David: "The earth is the LORD's, and everything in it. The world and all its people belong to him."[17]

It was mandated by Christ when he commissioned his followers to "go and make disciples of all the nations."[18]

It was revealed to John who wrote of a global vision of "a vast crowd, too great to count, from every nation and tribe and people and language" worshiping Jesus, the Lamb that ransomed people from every nation.[19] In heaven, there will be no bigotry or animosity, no racism, sexism, or ethnocentrism, no enmity or partiality, no disgust or dislike. Rather, humanity in all its diversity will worship in unity the one true living God for all eternity.

A World Upside Down Looks Up

Global and gospel history is happening now.

Before Russia invaded Ukraine in February 2022, Peter's church in the Donbas region was a church of about six hundred members. As the fighting intensified and casualties increased, people fled and the church dwindled until only a small group of twenty remained.

Like many pastors in the country, Peter was afraid, but his heart wouldn't let him leave his church. He risked his life to stay behind, knowing that at any moment his church might be targeted by a missile. Day and night, he labored to help people in need.

When the world turns upside down, people begin to look up, seeking peace, help, and at times, God. Paul wrote to the church in Thessalonica, a city that incited a riot because of the gospel, "You know of our concern for you from the way we lived when we were with you. So you received the message with joy from the Holy Spirit in spite of the severe suffering it brought you. . . . Our God gave us the courage to declare his Good News to you boldly, in spite of great opposition."[20]

Four months after the invasion, Peter's church grew from the twenty who stayed behind to two hundred people. Ukrainians who couldn't leave or didn't want to leave searched for help, and Peter and his church were there to give it. His testimony echoes that of the apostle Paul: "We loved you so much that we shared with you not only God's Good News but our own lives, too."[21]

Hope helps, and those who have hope step up and help those in need. God's mission is still in motion. The gospel is on the move. Missions history is being made today, around the world, and where you live.

Don't Live with a Someday Theology

We can make gospel history today. If that sounds like an over-inflated, romantic statement, remember that God is always at work and history is always happening. It's been said, "The best time to plant a tree was twenty years ago. The second-best time is today."[22] In other words, it's never too late to join God's history-making mission.

Most of us get caught in a whirlpool of what I call a "someday theology." We convince ourselves that we'll be involved in God's mission *someday*.

Someday, when I get older.

Someday, when I graduate.

Someday, when I have more money.

Someday, when I have more time.

Someday, when I get married.

Someday, when I have kids.

Someday, when the kids go to school.

Someday, when the kids move out.

Someday, when I retire.

Until someday never happens.

The apostle James warns, "Look here, you who say, 'Today or tomorrow we are going to a certain town and will stay there a year. We will do business there and make a profit.' How do you know what your life will be like tomorrow? Your life is like the morning fog—it's here a little while, then it's gone." James doesn't stop there. He goes on, turning up the heat: "Remember, it is sin to know what you ought to do and then not do it."[23]

Churches can get stuck in the sludge of someday thinking too. When my husband and I moved back to the US from Africa and planted a church that met in a school cafeteria for five years, we had a lot of someday thoughts regarding God's global mission and how our church fit into it.

Someday, when we have a building.

Someday, when we have a bigger budget.

Someday, when we have more staff.

Someday, when we have more members.

Someday thinking is a delusion, a slippery slope into no day at all. Eternity might be decades from now, or maybe tomorrow, or maybe in an hour. Who knows? But we have today. We have this moment to realign our aim with God's aim.

We realign our aim when we join with the God "who is able,

through his mighty power at work within us, to accomplish infinitely more than we might ask or think."[24] Consider that! God desires to do more than you can think up on your own. He longs to work in you and in your church in ways you don't even know to ask.

9

Eternal: What Matters Most

*If you live without a vision of the glory of God filling the
whole earth, you are in danger of serving your own dreams of
greatness as you wait to do "the next thing" God tells you.*

FLOYD MCCLUNG

HELL HAD A DOOR. Not knowing what I was entering, I walked
through it.

I had visited Hindu temples before—grand temples and decay-
ing ones—each one revered as a home for gods, devas, and avatars.
But this place was different. Death was in the open. I could see it,
smell it, and hear it.

At the Pashupatinath Temple in Kathmandu, Nepal, holy men
dressed in robes, painted their faces, and carried devilish pitchforks
as they roamed the tiered, concrete grounds. Dead bodies covered
with white and orange cloths were carried in and set on an incline
of steps so that their feet could be washed in the Bagmati River
before being placed on pyres and burned. Families wailed and
paid the holy men for prayers as ashes from the bodies fell into
the water, which they believed would carry the souls of their loved
ones downriver and into the next life.

It struck me that I was watching people go to hell.

I experienced quite a different atmosphere at another temple located 233 miles away and 12,100 feet up in the fresh air of the Himalayas. This temple was called Muktinath, which means "place of salvation." It is a sacred place for both Hindus and Buddhists.

At the temple, icy mountain water from a sacred river is channeled to flow continually through 108 fountains, each shaped like a bull's head mounted at the top of a long stone wall. In a streamlined fashion, people walk (or run, because it's so cold) beneath all the fountains. Here I watched people run around in search of salvation.

After one man finished his journey, I asked him, "Why do you walk under the waters? What is significant about them?"

"They wash away my sins," he said.

I paused when he said it, at a loss for words. Even now, as I type these words it seems as if there is no easy way to transition to what comes next. And maybe that's the point.

When facing the reality of how lost some people are, we shouldn't just skip to the next thing, as if eternity isn't real and their souls don't matter. Something I once heard David Platt say comes to mind: "We are often concerned the most with that which matters the least. And we are often concerned the least with that which matters the most."

Eternity matters the most.

Worth Dying For

If eternity matters the most, why don't we risk more to make Jesus known?

It's not because we don't value God and God's mission, but because we value something else more. We value what people might think. We value not being ridiculed. We value our safety. We value our time. We value our lives.

Risk requires exposing something of value to danger, threat, harm, or discomfort.

Before my husband and I moved overseas, a wise man told us, "Take whatever you want with you, but take it in your hand and not your heart." In other words, there's risk involved. Perhaps his statement exposes our problem.

Too often, we hold our faith in our hands and the things of this world in our hearts.

I'm not saying we don't hold tightly to Jesus. I believe many of us hold on with all our strength, not ever wanting to let go. But it's not our hands he wants to be in. He wants to be on the throne of our hearts.

Adoniram Judson was a pastor and missionary who risked everything. Gripped by both his love for a woman and his love for God's mission, he asked permission to marry Ann in a letter to her parents:

> I have now to ask whether you can consent to part with
> your daughter early next spring, to see her no more in
> this world? Whether you can consent to her departure . . .
> and her subjection to the hardships and sufferings of a
> missionary life? Whether you can consent to her exposure
> to the dangers of the ocean; to the fatal influence of the
> southern climate of India; to every kind of want and
> distress; to degradation, insult, persecution, and perhaps
> a violent death? Can you consent to all this, for the sake
> of Him who left His heavenly home and died for her and
> for you; for the sake of perishing, immortal souls; for the
> sake of Zion and the glory of God?[1]

Who says these kinds of things?

Let me give you another example.

In the 1950s, five men were tragically speared to death as they tried to bring the gospel to a remote tribe in Ecuador. Watching a documentary about these men, I heard words I'd never heard before from one of their widows, Elisabeth Elliot. She reminisced about the day her friend Nate Saint returned from a reconnaissance flight and announced, "I've found the Aucas," and the men began making plans to go meet them.

What she said next revealed the heart of a woman abandoned to God: "Don't you think it would make much better sense if a husband and wife with a baby would go down the river in a canoe? The Aucas certainly would not feel threatened by a man with his wife and baby. I'm willing to do it. Jim, are you willing to do it?" Her husband, Jim, said, "I think it's a great idea."[2]

These aren't people who were thrill seekers, adrenaline junkies, or the Navy SEALs of Christianity. So, where did such tenacity come from?

How do we live our lives not caring whether we live or die? How do we live for the good of others and for the glory of God? We have the answers in this statement from the apostle Paul: "And this is the secret: Christ lives in you. This gives you assurance of sharing his glory."[3]

Check Your Attitude

If we are part of something eternal, then we can't hold on to that which is temporal.

Did Esther not risk her life for the lives of others? "If I perish, I perish."[4]

Did Shadrach, Meshach, and Abednego not take risks? "If we are thrown into the blazing furnace, the God whom we serve is able to save us. . . . But even if he doesn't . . . we will never serve your gods."[5]

Did Paul not risk his life? "I am ready not only to be jailed at Jerusalem but even to die for the sake of the Lord Jesus."[6]

A decade ago, God led me to reconsider my life and the all-too-high value I placed on it when I read this familiar passage written by Paul:

> Have this mind among yourselves, which is yours in Christ Jesus, who, though he was in the form of God, did not count equality with God a thing to be grasped, but emptied himself, by taking the form of a servant, being born in the likeness of men. And being found in human form, he humbled himself by becoming obedient to the point of death, even death on a cross. Therefore God has highly exalted him and bestowed on him the name that is above every name, so that at the name of Jesus every knee should bow, in heaven and on earth and under the earth, and every tongue confess that Jesus Christ is Lord, to the glory of God the Father.[7]

You're likely so familiar with the passage that you may have skimmed it. If so, no judgment here. That's exactly what I did until God slowed me down. Unhurried, I considered what it meant for me to actually live it. That's when I decided to write out my personal version of Philippians 2:5-11:

> I will have this attitude in myself, which was also in Christ Jesus. Though I was born an American, can drive everywhere I go in my air-conditioned car, have running water when I want it, and have a comfortable bed in my more-than-adequate-square-footage home, I will not hold tightly in my heart to anything I am, to anything I

own, or to any plans I have for the future. I will give up my American and personal rights to become a servant to another culture. I will speak their language, walk like them, eat with them, sing their songs, dance their dances, live among them, and dress like them. I will humble myself to be less and lower than the people I serve so that I might be obedient to God, even if it means I must die a horrible death so they might know that Jesus Christ died for them, for God's glory.

Perhaps you should write your own version. The key is that you can't leave anything out, including death.

Start Where You Are

"Stop beating the same drum," my friend said. "You'll never draw a crowd if you always speak about God's mission." My friend wasn't wrong.

We were at a conference where I was asked to lead two break-out sessions. One was on God's mission and the other on anxiety. I've had experience in both subjects.

The breakout session on anxiety was packed to the point that people were sitting on the floor. In the breakout session on missions, only eight people showed up.

Participating in God's mission isn't something we do once until we figure out life. Spoiler alert: That never happens. God is work-ing in us, refining us so that he can use us to declare his story in every season of life.

Consider David, who wrote about being in a pit—a slimy, miry bog—that he couldn't get out of. Perhaps he attempted to claw his way out at some point, but he eventually surrendered his effort. As you read his words, notice who does what.

I waited patiently for the LORD;
  he inclined to me and *heard* my cry.
He drew me up from the pit of destruction,
  out of the miry bog,
and [*he*] *set my feet* upon a rock,
  making my steps secure.

PSALM 40:1-2, ESV, EMPHASIS ADDED

David prays, surrenders, and waits in the depths. But God hears, draws him up, and sets him in a secure place where he can walk again. But that is *not* the end of the story!

David goes on to state why God rescued him:

He put a new song in my mouth,
  a song of praise to our God.
Many will see and fear,
  and put their trust in the Lord.

PSALM 40:3, ESV, EMPHASIS ADDED

God works in us for the very purpose of making his name known. We're not the lead story of our lives—Jesus is! Paul said, "But my life is worth nothing to me unless I use it for finishing the work assigned me by the Lord Jesus—the work of telling others the Good News about the wonderful grace of God."[8]

The Most or the Least

What consumes your time and attention? That which matters most, or that which matters least?

The early church was a movement, and it had its messes. But I see that those in the church were a Jesus-exalting, gospel-sharing, people-baptizing, life-change-celebrating, disciple-making, church-planting, Bible-teaching, need-meeting, global-thinking, culture-crossing, audaciously-praying, boldly-going, generously-giving, strategically-sending, God-glorifying people.

It's a long list—and it's a convicting list.

Do an honest assessment. Skim the paragraph and consider which phrases describe you personally as well as those that describe your church.

While I'm tempted to give myself the benefit of the doubt, my calendar tells the unvarnished truth. My schedule, and that of other leaders I know, is probably better described by phrases such as event planning, team meeting, volunteer begging, digital marketing, ministry maintaining, worship band corralling, church building managing, errand running, strategic whiteboarding, crisis emailing, hardworking, often exhausting, and little fruit bearing.

Hear me say this—these are *not* bad things. But if the second list of activities isn't moving us toward the first list, which characterized the early church, I fear we are caught in the maintenance of church production and not in the mission of church reproduction. When ministry moves into maintenance mode, the mission suffers.

Eternal Focus

God is ushering in his Kingdom. He is unwaveringly, unchangingly, supremely passionate about his glory and committed to act for the sake of his name in all the earth. If we desire to align our life's ambition to God's mission, we need to be laser focused and farsighted with our vision.

- *Nearsighted*: Jesus loves me.
- *Farsighted*: Jesus loves me, and his love compels me to display and declare his love to others.

- *Nearsighted*: Jesus saved me.
- *Farsighted*: Jesus saved me and now sends me to tell of his salvation to others.

- *Nearsighted*: God so loved the world that he sent his only Son, Jesus.
- *Farsighted*: God so loved the world that he sent his only Son, Jesus—and Jesus sends me.

- *Nearsighted*: Church is where I gather with believers to worship God.
- *Farsighted*: Church is where I gather with believers to worship God so I can then go out into the community to lead others to worship the one true God who deserves praise from all people.

- *Nearsighted*: Jesus commissioned his followers to make disciples.
- *Farsighted*: Jesus commissioned his followers to make disciples of all nations.

Compelled by Love, Commissioned by a King

It's not that we love missions, but that we love God.

We don't go around the globe or into our city because we've talked ourselves into a deep love for people we've never met. We go because we have an all-consuming, burning, zealous love for God, whom those people have never met. John Stott wrote, "The highest of all missionary motives is neither obedience to the Great Commission (important as that is), nor love for sinners who are alienated and perishing . . . but rather zeal—burning and passionate zeal—for the glory of Jesus Christ."[9]

"Christ's love controls us," Paul wrote to the church in Corinth.[10] His love rends our hearts and seizes everything within us. His love is the driving force that compels us and propels us to make the message of his love known to others.

Why can't we just hang out with Christians? Because we are convinced that Christ died for all. If we believe this, it should burden us to live our lives in such a way that we throw down the rope of salvation to pull people out of the pit of hell. "He died for everyone," wrote the apostle Paul, "so that those who receive his new life will no longer live for themselves. Instead, they will live for Christ, who died and was raised for them."[11]

The love of Christ in us transforms how we see the world around us. Paul continued, "So we have stopped evaluating others from a human point of view. At one time we thought of Christ merely from a human point of view. How differently we know him now!"[12]

We don't just have information about Christ. We have words that are an invitation to a love relationship with Christ that results in life transformation—now and for eternity.

God is reconciling the world to himself through Jesus Christ. He has given us this message of reconciliation. We are sent as his ambassadors, commissioned with his message of reconciliation, and given authority to represent the King as he makes his appeal to others through us.[13]

Only for His Glory

God, in his love, prearranged to choose you and set you apart for
   something immeasurable,
   something biblical,
   something critical,
   something possible,

something radical,
something global,
something unstoppable,
something historical,
and something eternal.

You are part of something that is for, and only for, God's glory.
Glory is the aim of God's mission.
The earth is the arena of God's mission.
Nations are the scope of God's mission.
The church is the agent of God's mission.
Jesus' return is the end of God's mission.
Eternal life is the final result of God's mission.
As the church, this is your mission.
As a disciple, this is your mission.
You have a part to play in something bigger than you!

Notes

INTRODUCTION: YOU'RE PART OF SOMETHING BIGGER THAN YOU

1. Many Christians live in places around the world where it is dangerous or illegal to share the gospel. When caught, they may be arrested, jailed, fined, and sometimes ostracized by family.
2. Matthew 17:20-21.
3. Adapted from Lori McDaniel, "5 Shifts to Mobilize Your Church for Global Mission Involvement," Lifeway Research blog, September 24, 2019, https://lifewayresearch.com/2019/09/24/5-shifts-to-mobilize-your-church-for-global-mission-involvement/.
4. Acts 4:29-30, ESV, emphasis added.
5. Romans 5:5; 2 Corinthians 5:14-15.
6. Revelation 7:9, ESV.
7. Barna, *The Great Disconnect: Reclaiming the Heart of the Great Commission in Your Church* (Ventura, CA: Barna Group, 2022), 15.
8. Christopher J. H. Wright, *The Mission of God's People: A Biblical Theology of the Church's Mission* (Grand Rapids, MI: Zondervan, 2010), 19.
9. This statement is attributable to numerous sources. For an expanded version, see Christopher J. H. Wright, *The Mission of God: Unlocking the Bible's Grand Narrative* (Downers Grove, IL: IVP Academic, 2006), 22.
10. Exodus 4:2-4.
11. Exodus 4:4.
12. Dawson Trotman, *Born to Reproduce* (Colorado Springs: NavPress, 2018), 12.
13. Matthew 28:17.
14. Matthew 28:19.
15. Matthew 4:19.
16. Matthew 28:19; 2 Corinthians 5:20.
17. Though several online sites attribute this quote to William Carey (1761–1834), its authorship is unknown.
18. John 17:4.
19. 1 Thessalonians 2:12, adapted.

CHAPTER 1: IMMEASURABLE: THE ULTIMATE AIM OF GOD
1. Though often misattributed to Mark Twain and others, the original source is unknown.
2. Adoree Durayappah-Harrison, "The Spoiler Paradox: Knowing a Spoiler Makes a Story Better, Not Worse," *Psychology Today*, August 22, 2011, https://www.psychologytoday.com/us/blog/thriving101/201108/the -spoiler-paradox.
3. Scholar Daniel Akin writes, "This is a phrase used by Winston Churchill to describe Russia in the 1930s, but it applies just as well to John's apocalyptic vision." Daniel L. Akin, *Exalting Jesus In Revelation,* Christ-Centered Exposition Commentary, ed. David Platt, Daniel L. Akin, and Tony Merida (Nashville, TN: Holman Reference, 2016), 3.
4. Philippians 2:10-11.
5. Revelation 7:9, emphasis added.
6. Revelation 5:9, emphasis added.
7. Andreas J. Köstenberger and Peter T. O'Brien, *Salvation to the Ends of the Earth: A Biblical Theology of Mission* (Downers Grove, IL: InterVarsity, 2001), 263.
8. Jonathan Edwards, *Two Dissertations: I. Concerning the End for Which God Created the World, II. The Nature of True Virtue* (Boston: S. Kneeland, 1765), 109.
9. Revelation 21:23.
10. Revelation 15:4.
11. Köstenberger and O'Brien, *Salvation to the Ends of the Earth*, 262. Emphasis added.
12. Revelation 4:11, ESV.
13. Sura 6:100-101; Sura 4:156-157.
14. Job 42:3.
15. Romans 1:20.
16. 1 Kings 8:27.
17. Psalm 104:30-31.
18. Genesis 3:4.
19. Keith Whitfield, "The Triune God: The God of Mission," in *Theology and Practice of Mission: God, the Church, and the Nations,* ed. Bruce Riley Ashford (Nashville, TN: B&H, 2011), 18.
20. Isaiah 6:3.
21. Isaiah 6:5.
22. Isaiah 6:8.
23. Isaiah 26:8, NIV.

CHAPTER 2: BIBLICAL: GOD'S MANDATE IN ALL SCRIPTURE
1. Jedidiah Coppenger, "The Community of Mission: The Church," in *Theology and Practice of Mission: God, the Church, and the Nations,* ed. Bruce Riley Ashford (Nashville, TN: B&H, 2011), 60. Emphasis added.

2. Mark 1:17.
3. Matthew 22:29.
4. Luke 24:44-48, emphasis added. For the entire context, read Luke 24:27-48.
5. Psalm 46:10, emphasis added.
6. Christopher J. H. Wright, *The Mission of God: Unlocking The Bible's Grand Narrative* (Downers Grove, IL: IVP Academic, 2006), 23.
7. Many of the category headings here are from Preben Vang and Terry Carter, *Telling God's Story: The Biblical Narrative from Beginning to End* (Nashville, TN: B&H Academic, 2006).
8. Italics in the following Scripture quotations reflect the author's emphasis.
9. Habakkuk 2:14, ESV.
10. Genesis 9:1, ESV.
11. Christopher J. H. Wright, *The Mission of God's People: A Biblical Theology of the Church's Mission* (Grand Rapids, MI: Zondervan, 2010), 71.
12. Joshua 2:10-11.
13. Hebrews 1:3, NIV.

CHAPTER 3: CRITICAL: AN INCLUSIVE AND EXCLUSIVE GOSPEL
1. John 1:45.
2. Hebrews 1:3, NIV.
3. 1 John 4:10.
4. Romans 5:12. For context, read all of Romans 5.
5. Romans 5:15. For context, read all of Romans 5.
6. Daniel L. Akin, Benjamin L. Merkle, and George G. Robinson, *40 Questions About the Great Commission* (Grand Rapids, MI: Kregel Academic, 2020), 9.
7. See the Joshua Project at https://joshuaproject.net.
8. John 6:63.
9. John 14:6.
10. Matthew 7:13-14.
11. Mark 3:14, ESV, emphasis added.
12. Luke 10:20.
13. John 15:5, 8.
14. David J. Bosch, *Witness to the World: The Christian Mission in Theological Perspective* (Eugene, OR: Wipf and Stock, 2006), 81.
15. John 4:1-42.
16. John 4:7.
17. John 4:10.
18. John 4:16.
19. John 4:21.
20. John 4:26.
21. John 4:32, 34.

22. This definition of *worldview* comes from Zane Pratt, M. David Sills, and Jeff K. Walters in their book *Introduction to Global Missions* (Nashville, TN: B&H, 2014), 27.

23. John 4:35.

24. Dawson Trotman, *Born to Reproduce* (Colorado Springs: NavPress, 2018), 11, 13.

25. *National Study on Disciple Making in USA Churches: High Aspirations Amidst Disappointing Results*, Exponential and Grey Matter Research, March 2020, 3.

26. Kyle Idleman, *One at a Time: The Unexpected Way God Wants to Use You to Change the World* (Grand Rapids, MI: Baker, 2022), 179.

27. David Platt, *Radical: Taking Back Your Faith from the American Dream* (Colorado Springs: Multnomah, 2010), 104–105. Emphasis added.

CHAPTER 4: POSSIBLE: GOD'S MISSION WILL HAPPEN

1. John F. Kennedy, speech at Rice University, September 12, 1962. See the full transcript of the speech at https://boldfrontiers.blogs.rice.edu/home/speech-transcript/.

2. Kennedy, speech at Rice University.

3. Matthew 24:14, emphasis added.

4. Hudson Taylor, quoted in Daniel L. Akin, Benjamin L. Merkle, and George G. Robinson, *40 Questions About the Great Commission* (Grand Rapids, MI: Kregel Academic, 2020), 18.

5. Ralph D. Winter and Steven C. Hawthorne, eds., *Perspectives on the World Christian Movement: Reader and Study Guide*, 4th ed. (Pasadena, CA: William Carey Library, 2009), 37. "Mandates are not commands. By direct commands we assign small errands or daily chores. A mandate, on the other hand, releases authority and responsibility to pursue endeavors of historic importance. God has entrusted to Christ, and with Him to the Church, a mandate to fulfill His purpose for all history." See also the discussion titled "What Is the Great Commission?" in Akin, Merkle, and Robinson, *40 Questions*, 17–22.

6. John 17:4.

7. John 20:21.

8. John 17:20.

9. John 20:21-22.

10. John 14:12, 16-17.

11. Luke 24:13-45.

12. Luke 24:46-48.

13. For more information about Luke's version of the Great Commission, see Akin, Merkle, and Robinson, *40 Questions*, 185–186.

14. Mark 13:9-11.

15. Matthew 28:17.

16. Matthew 28:18-20.
17. "This passage contains only one verb in the imperative. There is one, and only one, command. That command is to make disciples. All the rest is commentary." Zane Pratt, "The Heart of the Task," *Discovering the Mission of God*, ed. Mike Barnett and Robin Martin (Downers Grove, IL: IVP Academic, 2012), 131.
18. Martin Luther, *On the Freedom of a Christian*, ed. and trans. Tryntje Helfferich (Indianapolis: Hackett, 2013), 38.
19. Psalm 71:15.
20. To learn more, see chapter 16 "Should the Verb 'Go/Going' Be Understood as a Command?" in Akin, Merkle, and Robinson, *40 Questions*, 147–153.
21. Genesis 12:3, NIV.
22. Revelation 7:9.
23. Winter and Hawthorne, *Perspectives*, 130.
24. Galatians 3:27.
25. Ephesians 4:5.
26. 1 Corinthians 12:13.
27. Matthew 28:20.
28. Pratt, "The Heart of the Task," *Discovering the Mission of God*, 134.
29. John 6:66.
30. David Platt, quoted in Paul J. Pastor, "David Platt: Reproducing Church, Transcendent Community—Part 1," *Outreach* magazine, October 21, 2020.
31. David Platt, "Great Commission Statistics That Should Concern Us," *Radical* (blog), May 5, 2021, https://radical.net/article/great-commission -statistics-that-should-concern-us/.
32. "What Is the 10/40 Window?" Joshua Project, undated, https://joshuaproject .net/resources/articles/10_40_window.
33. Barna defines "practicing Christians" as ones who attend church once a month or more, and who say their faith is important to them.
34. Barna, *The Great Disconnect: Reclaiming the Heart of the Great Commission in Your Church* (Ventura, CA: Barna Group, 2022), 16.
35. Barna, *The Great Disconnect*, 18.
36. Barna, *The Great Disconnect*, 20.
37. John Stam, graduation address, Moody Bible Institute, April 21, 1932.
38. John C. Stam, letter to China Inland Mission, December 6, 1934, accessed on Wayback Machine Internet Archive, https://web.archive.org/web /20161029093221/http://carlstam.org/familyheritage/images/J&BStam .letter.12.06.34.pdf.

CHAPTER 5: RADICAL: GOD'S UNUSUAL PLAN WITH UNLIKELY PEOPLE

1. John 6:53.

2. Acts 1:6.
3. Elisabeth Elliot, quoted in Ellen Vaughn, *Becoming Elisabeth Elliot* (Nashville, TN: B&H, 2020), 210.
4. Acts 2:1-3.
5. Acts 2:5-12.
6. Acts 2:41.
7. Charles Haddon Spurgeon, "The Golden Key of Prayer—Jer. 33:3," in *Spurgeon's Sermons: The Metropolitan Tabernacle Pulpit*, vol. 11 (1865), Classic Christian Library, 247. Emphasis added.
8. Romans 8:10-11, 26-27; 1 Corinthians 12:7-11; John 16:7-8, 13-15; John 14:26.
9. Numbers 11:25, emphasis added.
10. Numbers 24:2-3, emphasis added.
11. 1 Samuel 10:10, emphasis added.
12. Ezekiel 11:5, emphasis added.
13. Luke 1:41-42, emphasis added.
14. Luke 1:67, emphasis added.
15. Acts 4:8, emphasis added.
16. Acts 4:31, emphasis added.
17. Acts 2:16-17, emphasis added.
18. Matthew 26:69-75; Acts 2:14-41.
19. Luke 9:51-56; Acts 8:14-25.
20. Matthew 28:19-20.
21. Acts 8:26.
22. Acts 8:26-38.
23. Acts 10:19-20.
24. Acts 10:34-35.
25. Acts 16:6-8.
26. Acts 16:9.
27. Acts 4:13.
28. Acts 3:4.
29. Luke 19:1-4; John 5:1-6; Luke 13:10-13; Luke 5:12-13.
30. Acts 3:6.
31. Acts 3:8.
32. Acts 3:16, 19.
33. Acts 4:4.
34. Christopher J. H. Wright, *The Mission of God: Unlocking the Bible's Grand Narrative* (Downers Grove, IL: IVP Academic, 2006), 319.
35. John 14:13, emphasis added.
36. Acts 4:12, emphasis added.
37. Matthew 28:19, emphasis added.
38. Philippians 2:10-11, emphasis added.

39. Colossians 3:17, ESV, emphasis added.
40. If you've never witnessed demon possession, you might question this story. I understand. I debated whether to include it. But here's why I did: The enemy is real, and he seeks to destroy people's lives. He is at work in your surroundings, and he is at work in other parts of the globe.
41. Mark 5:15, NIV.
42. Luke 10:3, 4, 7.

CHAPTER 6: GLOBAL: TO THE ENDS OF THE EARTH

1. Ed Stetzer, foreword to Steve Addison, *What Jesus Started: Joining the Movement, Changing the World* (Downers Grove, IL: InterVarsity, 2012), 12.
2. Oswald J. Smith, quoted in Daniel L. Akin, Benjamin L. Merkle, and George G. Robinson, *40 Questions About the Great Commission*, (Grand Rapids, MI: Kregel Academic, 2020), 109.
3. Acts 2:7, 11.
4. Acts 6:10, NIV.
5. John 15:20.
6. Mark 13:9.
7. Acts 8:1.
8. Acts 8:4.
9. Mark 5:5.
10. Mark 5:10.
11. Mark 5:13.
12. Mark 5:15, 18-20.
13. John 4:28-30, 39, 42.
14. Christopher J. H. Wright, *The Mission of God: Unlocking the Bible's Grand Narrative* (Downers Grove, IL: IVP Academic, 2006), 403–404.
15. Acts 17:26-27, NIV.
16. Ralph Winter, quoted on E4 Project website, https://www.e4project .org/about/e4-process/educate/.
17. American Immigration Council, "Immigrants in the United States" Fact Sheet, September 21, 2021, https://www.americanimmigrationcouncil.org /research/immigrants-in-the-united-states. Abby Budiman, "Key Findings about US Immigrants," Pew Research Center, August 20, 2020, https:// www.pewresearch.org/fact-tank/2020/08/20/key-findings-about-u-s -immigrants/. "Missions Stats: The Current State of the World," The Traveling Team, November 2021, http://www.thetravelingteam.org/stats. "Why is Well-Managed, Legal Immigration Significant to the United States?," US Department of State, https://www.state.gov/other-policy -issues/international-migration/. "SEVIS by the Numbers: Annual Report on International Student Trends," US Immigration and Customs Enforcement, 2021, https://www.ice.gov/doclib/sevis/pdf/sevisBTN2021.pdf.

18. Romans 5:8, emphasis added.
19. Matthew 5:43-45.
20. Leviticus 19:33-34.
21. Luke 10:36-37.
22. Deuteronomy 24:19.
23. Exodus 23:9.
24. Matthew 25:35.
25. John 13:35.
26. Romans 12:9.
27. Caleb Crider, Larry McCrary, Rodney Calfee, and Wade Stephens, *Tradecraft: For the Church on Mission* (Louisville, KY: Upstream Collective, 2013, 2017), 71.
28. Acts 17:22-23.
29. Acts 17:17.
30. Acts 17:32.
31. Acts 17:27.

CHAPTER 7: UNSTOPPABLE: A CHURCH BEYOND BORDERS AND BARRIERS
1. "The Full Story of Thailand's Extraordinary Cave Rescue," BBC, July 14, 2018, https://www.bbc.com/news/world-asia-44791998.
2. "Global Dashboard," Joshua Project, 2022, https://joshuaproject.net/people_groups/statistics.
3. Acts 13:1-3.
4. Timothy Keller and John Stott, quoted in Tony Merida, *Exalting Jesus in Acts,* Christ-Centered Exposition Commentary, ed. David Platt, Daniel L. Akin, and Tony Merida (Nashville, TN: Holman Reference, 2017), 155.
5. Acts 11:20-21.
6. 1 Corinthians 3:9.
7. Romans 10:13.
8. Romans 10:14-15, emphasis added.
9. Merida, *Exalting Jesus in Acts*, 166.
10. Acts 13:3.
11. Luke 6:12-16.
12. John 20:21.
13. Peter J. Morden, *Offering Christ to the World: Andrew Fuller (1754–1815) and the Revival of Eighteenth Century Particular Baptist Life* (Waynesboro, GA: Paternoster, 2004), 136.
14. Morden, *Offering Christ to the World*.
15. Romans 15:20.
16. David Platt, "Great Commission Statistics That Should Concern Us,"

Radical (blog), May 5, 2021, https://radical.net/article/great-commission
-statistics-that-should-concern-us/.

17. William J. Danker, *Profit for the Lord: Economic Activities in Moravian Missions and the Basel Mission Trading Company* (Eugene, OR: Wipf and Stock, 1971), 13, 73.
18. 2 Corinthians 1:11.
19. John Piper, *Let the Nations Be Glad! The Supremacy of God in Missions*, 3rd ed. (Grand Rapids, MI: Baker Academic, 2010), 65.
20. Andrew Murray, *The Key to the Missionary Problem* (London: James Nisbet, 1902), 152.
21. Andrew Murray, quoted in Center for Mission Mobilization, *Xplore: Discover God's Word, God's World, and God's Work*, 2nd ed. (Fayetteville, AR: CMM Press, 2020).
22. Colossians 4:3-4.
23. Romans 10:1.
24. Matthew 9:38.
25. Romans 15:20.
26. 2 Thessalonians 3:1.
27. 2 Corinthians 4:8-9, 12, 15-16.
28. Acts 14:3.
29. 2 Corinthians 8:2-3, ESV.
30. Platt, "Great Commission Statistics That Should Concern Us."
31. "Missions Stats: The Current State of the World," The Traveling Team, November 2021, http://www.thetravelingteam.org/stats.
32. Note that I'm intentionally *not* using the term "volunteer teams," as there are no volunteers in God's mission. God's mission *is* our mission.
33. Philippians 1:5.
34. 2 Corinthians 5:11, 13-14.
35. John G. Paton, *John G. Paton, Missionary to the New Hebrides: An Autobiography* (New York: Robert Carter & Brothers, 1889), 91–92.

CHAPTER 8: HISTORICAL: THE STATE OF THE WORLD
1. Steve Addison, *Movements That Change the World: Five Keys to Spreading the Gospel*, rev. ed. (Downers Grove, IL: InterVarsity, 2011), 42.
2. Ruth A. Tucker, *From Jerusalem to Irian Jaya: A Biographical History of Christian Missions* (Grand Rapids, MI: Zondervan, 2004), 100.
3. "Missions Stats: The Current State of the World," The Traveling Team, November, 2021, http://www.thetravelingteam.org/stats.
4. Lesslie Newbigin, quoted in Ruth A. Tucker, *From Jerusalem to Irian Jaya*, 13.
5. Acts 19:21-41.
6. Matthew 16:18, ESV.

7. John R. W. Stott, "The Living God Is a Missionary God," https://docslib
.org/doc/2484766/the-living-god-is-a-missionary-god. Taken from *You Can
Tell the World*, ed. James E. Berney (Downers Grove, IL: InterVarsity, 1979).

8. Steve Addison, *What Jesus Started: Joining the Movement, Changing the
World* (Downers Grove, IL: InterVarsity, 2012), 15.

9. Zane Pratt, M. David Sills, and Jeff K. Walters, *Introduction to Global
Missions* (Nashville, TN: B&H Publishing Group, 2014), 101.

10. Ramsay MacMullen, quoted in Tucker, *From Jerusalem to Irian Jaya*, 17.

11. Kenneth Scott Latourette, quoted in Pratt, Sills, and Walters, *Introduction to
Global Missions*, 103.

12. Ryan Shaw, *Rethinking Global Mobilization: Calling the Church to Her Core
Identity* (Armstrong, MO: Ignite Media, 2022), 157.

13. Todd M. Johnson, "The 100-year Shift of Christianity to the South,"
Gordon Conwell Theological Seminary, October 9, 2019, https://www
.gordonconwell.edu/blog/the-100-year-shift-of-christianity-to-the-south/.

14. Shaw, *Rethinking Global Mobilization*, xv. Italics in the original.

15. Psalm 22:27.

16. Genesis 1:28, ESV.

17. Psalm 24:1.

18. Matthew 28:19.

19. Revelation 7:9; Revelation 5:9.

20. 1 Thessalonians 1:5-6; 2:2.

21. 1 Thessalonians 2:8.

22. Chinese proverb, quoted in Addison, *Movements That Change the World*, 84.

23. James 4:13-14, 17.

24. Ephesians 3:20.

CHAPTER 9: ETERNAL: WHAT MATTERS MOST

1. Daniel L. Akin, *Ten Who Changed the World* (Nashville, TN: B&H, 2012), 17.

2. Elisabeth Elliot, interviewed in *Beyond the Gates of Splendor*, a documentary
about the five missionaries who were killed while attempting to contact
the Huaorani tribe in Ecuador in 1956. The documentary was written
and directed by Jim Hanon, produced by Bearing Fruit Productions, and
distributed by Every Tribe Entertainment (2002).

3. Colossians 1:27.

4. Esther 4:16, ESV.

5. Daniel 3:17-18.

6. Acts 21:13.

7. Philippians 2:5-11, ESV.

8. Acts 20:24.

9. John R. W. Stott, *The Message of Romans* (Downers Grove, IL: InterVarsity, 1994), 53.
10. 2 Corinthians 5:14.
11. 2 Corinthians 5:15.
12. 2 Corinthians 5:16.
13. 2 Corinthians 5:18-21.

About the Author

Lori McDaniel is a multifaceted leader, conference speaker, and Bible teacher. Her passion for discipleship among nations has taken her to more than thirty countries to work with indigenous leaders and cross-cultural missionaries. She served for a time in Africa as a missionary and worked with the International Mission Board as manager of marketing and mobilization. She and her husband, Mike, live in northwest Arkansas, where he is the lead pastor of the church they planted. Lori has extensive experience in women's ministry and church strategy. She holds an MA in intercultural studies from Southeastern Baptist Theological Seminary.

If you liked this book, you'll want to get involved in

Church Equip!

Do you have a desire to learn more about serving God through your local church?

Would you like to see how God can use you in new and exciting ways?

Get your church involved in Church Equip, an online ministry designed to prepare church leaders and church members to better serve God's mission and purpose.

Check us out at **ChurchEquip.com**